The Godswept Heart

For my parents
who gave me my first lessons
in family life

The Godswept Heart

Parables of Family Life by
Marcia Hollis
with prayers by
Reginald Hollis
and illustrations by
Vera Semple

SEABURY · NEW YORK

1982

The Seabury Press
815 Second Avenue
New York, N.Y. 10017

Printed in Canada

ISBN 0-8164-2410-1

Contents

Preface

As a way of coping with the science requirement in my first year at university, I found myself (having no talent for things mathematical) in an introductory geography course. It was a long time ago, but I can clearly remember the cheerful manner in which our professor introduced us to cloud formations, rock formations, and land formations. Whatever other formations there may have been are now lost to my mind.

However, two things that he said in that class stand out in my memory. On the first occasion, the professor was attempting to describe a particular piece of rock, which had bits of another rock imbedded in it. "It looks," he said thoughtfully, "a little bit like *Chipits*." At the time it struck me as strange that a man would make that comparison, because most men don't really know about Chipits. They know about chocolate chip cookies, which is the form in which they usually encounter Chipits.

A few weeks later the second incident occurred. The professor was trying to give us an impression of a particular hill formation. Here he said, "They look something like an upside-down *Pyrex* bowl." Now every woman in North America undoubtedly knows those ubiquitous sets of mixing bowls produced by Pyrex. At that time they came in a set of blue, red, green, and yellow bowls of graduated sizes, and since there were very few other mixing bowls of the nesting variety available, they probably had the market cornered. But the point is: why was this man using what are in fact the technical terms of a housewife's profession to talk about science?

These two incidents stuck in my mind, and when, a year or so later, I happened to be at a party with some graduate geography students who were talking about my old professor, I was more than a little interested. The discussion had turned to field trips, and I asked with a sudden flash of inspiration, "Tell me, does that professor take his wife on field trips?"

"He's the only one who does," they said. "How did you know?"

The point about all this is that we bring to our observation and understanding of any subject an outlook or viewpoint which is conditioned by our own experience of life. My geography professor took his wife on field trips, and probably some of her observations about rock formations stayed with him. If she had declined to go on field trips, his comparisons might have been quite different.

The same principle applies to theology. Since the earliest days of the church until now, biblical exegesis and study have been left almost entirely in the hands of men. And they have predominately been *unmarried* men, whose total experience of family life has been limited to their childhood years. As a result their outlook in interpreting the scriptures has been almost exclusively masculine. This does not imply that what they have said or written has no validity. It simply means that a whole dimension of human experience has been largely ignored in our understanding of the Bible.

Now that women have begun to study theology, more attention is being paid to the role of women in the Bible. Women scholars are attuned to matters of feminine concern in a way that men never have been. It's not a question of chauvinism. It is just the natural order of things. Jesus somehow seemed to rise above the natural distinctions of sex. For the most part, he was a man speaking to men about money and productivity, about law and taxes, about sheep-herding and vine-dressing. But mixed in with all these items of masculine interest were pithy comments about yeast and lamps and patching clothes.

We all need to strive for this broader view of life. We need to learn from each other. A book of meditations by a home-maker is not necessarily written just for home-makers, and I hope that people in other walks of life will find it helpful too. This book is, in a way, a record of God's action in my life over the last twenty years as I have gone about the very ordinary tasks of keeping house and raising a family. It's about cooking and cleaning and watching kids grow up. From my own perspective, it's about God letting himself be known in even the dullest activity, and thereby putting his own shining finish on it.

The Godswept Heart

A friend of mine lost her diamond engagement ring and spent hours searching the house for it with no success, until suddenly she remembered leaving it beside the kitchen sink when she had been washing dishes. Reasoning that it might have fallen into the drain, she called a plumber as a last desperate hope, and sure enough, when he had taken the pipes apart, there was her ring in the trap. She was so excited that she gave the plumber a hug, told her husband to bring home some wine, dug a fancy casserole out of the freezer, and invited all their friends over for dinner.

If Jesus had been telling the parable of the lost coin today, he might have told it that way. It doesn't seem to make much difference to us. . .the loss of a silver coin. I certainly wouldn't turn the house upside down for a dime or a quarter. Scholars have suggested that the ten silver coins formed part of the woman's dowry, and so they inevitably assumed an importance beyond their mere financial value, although what with inflation, their value then was considerably more than now. In a way they may have been the Palestinian equivalent of an engagement ring.

There are three parables about the kingdom of heaven in the fifteenth chapter of the Gospel according to Saint Luke. They are the parables of the good shepherd, the lost coin, and the prodigal son, in that order. We know them well, particularly the first and third parables, because preachers, evangelists and writers of devotional books have made such a lot of them. The common theme is the joy in heaven over one repentent sinner.

The parable of the good shepherd is usually taken to represent Jesus going out into the dark night of a sinful world to save one lost lamb. In John's Gospel Jesus actually said, "I am the good shepherd." So we know this is not a faulty analogy. The parable of the prodigal son represents the Father welcoming home a sinful but repentant son. We understand from this that our heavenly Father will give us the same joyful welcome when we turn to him from our sinful ways.

Father, Son . . . and then what? Smack in the middle of those two stories is the parable about a woman sweeping her house. She lost a coin, a valuable coin, and then she swept and searched diligently until she found it. We probably have no trouble realizing that any one of us could be the coin in that parable, but somehow there has been a reluctance to identify that sweeping woman with God.

Sweep, sweep. I can imagine her without any difficulty. I too use a broom, particularly in country cottages where we don't have the luxury of a vacuum cleaner. There are ridiculous things to lose like car keys, earrings, and yes, my engagement ring. And then of course, the cottage has to be cleaned up before you leave. The dust rises and settles again, the heavy furniture has to be moved so that you can sweep underneath and not just around it, and amazing little treasures turn up, like bits of crayon and a toy that was lost last summer but somehow got missed in the final cleaning.

I like to think of that sweeping woman, looking for her lost coin. I have the feeling that no corners will be cut, that every bed will be turned, that every chair will be moved, until finally the lost piece of silver comes to light. God doesn't give up on us either.

To do a really thorough job of sweeping a room, you have to tidy it first. Old newspapers in the corner are bundled up and put in the garbage. Odd shoes and stray toys are collected and put in their respective cupboards. Little tables with fragile knick-knacks are moved to another room. In the old days, when housewives still went in for orgies of spring cleaning, even the carpets would be rolled up and taken outside for beating. All the non-essentials are removed so that nothing gets in the way of sweeping up all the dirt and dust.

Sometimes we pray: "Make a clean heart within me, O God," or words to that effect, but never stop to think that we might do a little tidying up on our own. Sometimes God uses circumstances, and we find that a certain activity, useful or otherwise, is suddenly closed to us. Like the knick-knacks, it may not have been dirty in itself, but it was getting in the way of the cleaning process. We are to be single-hearted in loving God and our neighbour. Jesus said, "Seek first the kingdom of God and his righteousness, and all else shall be added unto you." *Seek first the kingdom of God.* This is the secret of a clean heart, to look for God's presence and God's will in every aspect of our daily lives. Everything else takes second place. "Thou shalt have no other gods before me," is the first commandment.

The Bible uses different metaphors to express the activity of God. Jesus talked about a shepherd, a father, and a sweeping woman. He also spoke about wind in relation to the Holy Spirit, and this comparison is used throughout the scriptures. In Hebrew the word *ruach* is used for both 'wind' and 'spirit.' When the prophet Isaiah talks about the Holy Spirit of God, he is using a word which also means wind. When Jesus wanted to explain the action of the Holy Spirit to Nicodemus, he said, "The wind blows where it wills, and you hear the sound of it, but you do not know whence it comes or whither it goes; so it is with everyone who is born of the Spirit."

Wind can be gentle or strong. A faint breeze may barely stir the leaves in a tree, and yet a few hours later a raging storm may blow the same tree right over on its side. A soft wind cools us in the heat, dries the clothes on the line, and spreads about the pollen which enables plants to grow, but wind may also be destructive when an unexpected tornado levels everything in its path.

Wind has a powerful erosive effect. Given a clear area to sweep across, it can blow almost continuously against a stretch of coastline or across a plain. Young trees reach maturity dwarfed and stunted, and any outcropping of rock or plateau is slowly, patiently, inevitably levelled. Both the Psalmist and Jesus must have known this kind of desert wind. They were both familiar with great open hills and windswept landscapes. Such places have their own deep spiritual influence on us. From the top of a mountain, in the broad reach of a desert, by the pounding surf of the ocean, or simply beneath the night time expanse of open sky, we become aware of the littleness of our own affairs and ambitions, and of the all-prevailing majesty of God.

We ask God for a clean heart, and what we really want is a Godswept heart, with clear views of the real issues in life. We want his Spirit, his wind, to blow through our lives, taking with it the tumbledown shacks of self-importance, and the dry leaves of the unforgiven past. We want the deadwood of unfruitful activity knocked out of our trees so that we can get on with new growth. We want that woman with her broom to come and sweep, to drive away the dust of our wrong-doing, to get everything spick and span and spotless. And all to what purpose?

It's an awful thing to admit, but my house gets cleaned up when I'm getting ready for company. And I suppose that's as good a reason as any to have a clean heart. "Blessed are the clean in heart," said Jesus, "for they shall see God." When our heart has been swept and garnished, we can't leave it empty. We must love something or someone. We are made to love, and specifically we are made to love God, although the nature of love is such that he can't force it. Loving God is a commandment, and therefore we know it is possible. It is *the* commandment, and therefore we know it is necessary. God loved the world so much that he gave his only-begotten son, and we want to love him in return. But this is only truly possible when the heart is clean.

The staggering promise of scripture is that God himself in the Holy Spirit will make his dwelling place with us. He who was willing to be born in a stable is just as ready to be welcomed in the most stained and dusty heart among us, but we have to be prepared for him to clean us up when he comes. Otherwise he won't stay. "O God, make clean our hearts within us," we pray with the Psalmist, "and take not thy Holy Spirit from us." The Holy Spirit is a purifying, cleansing force, like a wind sweeping across a plain, or a woman sweeping with her broom. Lord, give me a Godswept heart.

O God
I gave myself to you,
but I know there's still
clutter in my heart,
things to which I'm attached,
plans and ambitions which I won't let go,
and hidden guilt of which I'm ashamed.
There are areas of commitment
covered with dust
and almost forgotten.
It's time for a spring clean,
to blow out the cobwebs of self-deception,
for my heart will never be clean
till it's swept
by You.

Father and Mother

As a very little girl my biggest ambition was to become a mother. The future father was a somewhat nebulous part of the picture, but I fully intended to have twenty children and bake cookies every day. In the meantime, like the other little girls on my street, I practised by playing house. We dressed our dolls and had tea parties. We changed diapers and walked our "babies," and sometimes we spanked them too. And every night we tucked our children into bed. We were very good mothers.

Of course we grew up and those ambitions faded away. We realized that housework is dirty and demeaning, and that even the best mother is "just a housewife" unless she has some other job. My friends and I flitted from one career option to another through high school. The only really boring subject was domestic science. (Do they still offer it?) Nobody wanted to be a drudge, even an educated one.

By the time we reached university, I had more or less settled upon a type of work which promised a fairly exciting future. A year in London was part of the plan, and then another stint in Paris or Rome. There was the possibility of living in the Middle East for a stretch, and then eventually a return home, where with all that experience, a top-ranking job would undoubtedly be waiting for me. Youth has boundless optimism.

The hitch to all these lovely plans came when I met my future husband. He was the university chaplain, and in a well-meaning effort to warn me of the difficulties of being a minister's wife, told me that he was thinking of going to teach in a theological college in Japan. It struck me as a way of having the best of both worlds. What are plans for, if you can't be flexible? We were married the following autumn.

As it turned out, the theological college in Japan never materialized. The last thing I ever wanted to be was a suburban housewife, but after five years of living in a downtown apartment with a new baby arriving every other year, one's perspective has a way of changing. The offer of a suburban church was too good to resist, especially since it included a nice split-level rectory with a garden.

That first winter, with snow piled four feet high outside the front door, was a long one. My husband was busy looking after the needs of a fast-growing community. Like other young mothers, I found myself isolated for long periods of the day without any adult contact. In the city, I had managed to carry a part-time job which gave me an outside interest. Where we now lived, there was no opportunity to work in my particular field, and even if there had been, it was impossible to find a daytime babysitter.

In my loneliness I turned to prayer and discovered that God really is a friend. And in that growing relationship, I made another discovery. Until then my dealings with God had always been on the level of a child talking to her Father. Now I found that we also communicated on the level of one parent talking to another. There were times when I might be concerned with some particular fault in my children, and then I'd realize that God had the same fault to deal with in me. It gave me an entirely new outlook on life.

One of the things I realized was that God may be a Father, but he's certainly a very liberated one. He does things for us that no self-respecting male chauvinist would dream of doing. He feeds us, cleans up our messes, watches over all our activities, and then gives us a good washing when we come to him all dirty from whatever we have been doing. That's the kind of work mothers do. It was a very encouraging thought.

In the Old Testament I discovered that God is described as both father *and* mother. There aren't many such references, but enough to make one think. Moses, speaking to the Children of Israel, said, "You were unmindful of the Rock that begot you, and you forgot the God who gave you birth." Describing the new life which would come to Israel, the prophet Isaiah saw God as a woman in labour: "For a long time I have held my peace, I have kept still and restrained myself; but now I will cry out like a woman in travail, I will gasp and pant." Giving birth is a woman's function, just about the only one that is uniquely hers and which no man can do. Yet here was the great Lord of heaven quite willing to be identified with this role.

As Christians we talk quite easily about being "born again," and forget that this is the work of the Holy Spirit. Jesus himself said, "That which is born of the flesh is flesh, and that which is born of the spirit is spirit."

Man is born of woman, and not the other way around. A mother gives birth and not the father. When Jesus told Nicodemus about the work of the Holy Spirit, he left the church with a teaching that a patriarchal society was unable to absorb. God, through the action of the Holy Spirit, is also our Mother.

The basic concept of a father has to include a mother, just as the concept of a mother has to include a father. Logically it doesn't make sense that Jesus would teach us to think of God as a heavenly father unless we also had a heavenly mother. Patriarchal society or not, wherever the direct commandment of God is concerned in the scriptures, mothers are always included with fathers. "Thou shalt honour thy father *and thy mother*." "Whoever curses his father *or his mother. . .*" "For this cause shall a man leave his father *and his mother. . .*"

The thought of God as a mother as well as a father was not completely unknown in the early days of the church. Clement of Alexandria, a saintly second-century theologian and Father of the Church, wrote: "The Word is all things to the infant; father, mother, tutor, and nurse." But at the same time, the early Christians were in the forefront of a battle against the abuses of ancient worship, the debased emphasis on sexual relationships among the gods and goddesses, and the inevitable cult prostitution that accompanied it. The worship of the earth goddess with her fertility symbolism could not be allowed a toe-hold in Christianity any more than it had been allowed in Judaism. How deeply rooted such worship was can be seen in the way the earth goddess lingers on in our folklore, even after nineteen centuries of Christianity.

It disturbs me to hear Christian women glibly telling their children about "Mother Earth" and "Mother Nature." To talk in this way is a desecration of the nature which God has given us, and yet I did it myself for years without ever considering the implications. Comforting a child with a scraped knee, I might put a dressing over the cut and say, "Now we'll just leave it to Mother Nature." Even in church, I would happily sing that beautiful hymn which invites "all creatures of our God and King" to give praise and honour to the creator – the burning sun, the silver moon, the rushing wind, and finally

> "Dear mother earth, who day by day
> Unfoldest blessing on our way. . ."

What hidden message are we giving a child who is taught in one breath about "Our Father in Heaven," and in the next breath about "Mother Earth"? God created mankind in his own image. "Male and female, created he them." Nowhere in the Bible do we read that women have been modelled on anything but their creator. "Mother Earth" is as demeaning to the true nature of womanhood as it ever was in those long-gone Temples of Ashtoreth against which the prophets of Israel raged. It equates women with the earth and the things of the earth, with fertility and good harvest. The church has always stood against that.

Our parentage is in heaven, for we are spiritual beings. God is our father and God is also our mother. The basis for this understanding of the parental nature of God has always been present in the scriptures. Only recently, however, have theologians of many different backgrounds been led to think about it in depth, so that even Pope John Paul I, speaking at a regular Sunday Angelus blessing in Saint Peter's Square not long before he died, said: "He is Father. Even more, God is Mother, who does not wish to harm us."

Having recognized this, it doesn't matter that we talk about God as *he* or *him* as long as we don't let this lead us into the semantic trap of supposing that God is somehow exclusively male. God must contain within himself both the very essence of manhood and the very essence of womanhood, for it is we who are made in his image and not the other way around.

It certainly doesn't mean that we suddenly need to begin addressing some of our prayers to *Our Heavenly Mother.* This would go against the very nature of God, against the Unity which knows no division. Sly children will sometimes try to play one parent off against another, but there is no room for that with the One who knows our very being. We have been told to pray to our Father in heaven and that is what we should continue to do.

When our children were little, I noticed that one would sometimes run into the house yelling, "Mom!" and if I happened to be on the phone, my husband would automatically answer, "Yes, what is it?" Just as frequently, it would happen the other way around and I would respond to a night-time cry of "Dad!" because I was already awake and my husband was sound asleep. And it never mattered at all to the children when this happened because what the cry really meant was, "Parent!" I think this is what happens when we pray to our heavenly Father. It is a term of relationship which God himself has taught us to use. And yet, just as clearly, he has given us cause to know that God is also our Mother.

O God
When I think I've
got you typed
in some set of words,
keep expanding my vision.
You're my father,
you're my mother,
but you're always more.
Always beyond me,
draw me to reach out
not to concepts
but to You.

"We were very good mothers" — *Father and Mother.*

Baby Talk

Every young mother's Baby Book points up the highlights of infancy, the moments that she wants to record for posterity. Most changes take place gradually, but some developments happen all at once. There is the appearance of the first tooth, the day baby sat up by himself, the first step, and probably most exciting of all, the first words. The day a baby begins to make intelligible sounds is the day he really begins to communicate.

It takes about three years for a young child to learn to talk and develop a basic vocabulary. What an accomplishment it is! Not only does he have to learn the words themselves, he has to grasp the use of language – that certain symbols (in this case, sounds) represent objects, people, actions, desires, and feelings. Just to make things more difficult, the baby has had no previous experience of people, actions, or feelings before he has to start learning the language for them. When a new baby begins to learn to talk, it is not in the least comparable to a high school student beginning the study of a foreign language like French. The student already knows how to talk. He knows what a pen is, even if he doesn't know the French word for it, and therefore it is a relatively simple matter to substitute *la plume* for the pen when he is speaking. But the young baby first has to learn what a pen is – that it is small and hard and cylindrical, that it makes marks, that it can be chewed on but not swallowed. All this has to be part of a baby's experience before he can understand the word *pen*.

No wonder young babies spend such a lot of time crying. How frustrating it would be to have intense feelings of hunger, loneliness, and even fear, and to be totally unable to express ourselves in any meaningful way. And how much worse it is to be unable to put a name to these feelings, or even to identify what is troubling us. We have to run a similar obstacle course when we first begin to pray. As new-born Christians we are faced with learning a new language, God's language. And it is as difficult for us to learn to speak in this new manner as it is for a baby to learn that different sounds express his needs and feelings.

Prayer begins at this elementary level for most people. We turn to God with our needs, hopes, and frustrations, and we are a little bit like the two-year old who says, "Me hungry now," or "Daddy come soon?" or "Don't wanna go bed." It's communication alright, but on a very one-sided basis. The two-year old doesn't really care to hear why he can't have cookies half an hour before dinner, or that bedtime is early because he is just getting over pneumonia. Even if he did listen, he wouldn't understand the mechanics of cookies spoiling an appetite, or what pneumonia and lowered resistance really mean. His mother can tell him, but he won't have the vocabulary or experience to understand what she is saying until he is considerably older.

In the same way, we simply don't understand or even hear a lot of what God tells us. We find ourselves groping for answers and explanations, and then not understanding or recognizing them when they come, like the young child who doesn't understand *why* he has to go to bed early or *why* he can't bring baby gerbils into the bathtub. It's frustrating for young mothers to be constantly answering questions when it's obvious that the answers are not understood, and the persistent *why* of suffering mankind must be equally frustrating to God.

Just as young children learn to talk and understand by living with their parents, so we learn to understand God by living with him. It's a slow process. There isn't a language in the world that you can pick up overnight, no matter how Berlitz and other language schools may advertise. To understand a language and a culture, you need to live in it, to be immersed in it. In just that way, we need to live with God and to be immersed in his Spirit. Only then do we begin to understand what he is really trying to tell us and how he really wants us to live.

Living with God has to be a 24 hour a day experience, but it's a good idea to take some of that time to focus our hearts and understanding directly on him and his will for us. Regular Bible reading and prayer are the hallmarks of the mature Christian, and we can never hope to progress in the spiritual life without them. Sometimes the practice of a quiet time is immediately and obviously helpful. I have known people who spoke of it almost as a briefing period, when God gave them their marching orders for the day. This was never the way my own quiet time worked, but then God treats all his children differently. Catherine Marshall once said that her own special insights seldom came during her prayer time, but rather when she was occupied with some mundane household task like ironing. This may be how it is for most people. When we deliberately set aside a daily time to spend with God, he lets us know his presence at other unexpected moments too.

There is a lot of psychological talk these days about body language and other forms of non-verbal communication. There is a recognition that words alone almost never mean everything that we want them to say. Sometimes it's difficult enough just to describe a simple material object. How much harder it is to express your depth of feeling when a friend's husband is killed in a hunting accident. The mere words "I'm sorry" hardly express your real compassion. Or again, what words are adequate to thank a man who saved your child from drowning?

When we talk to God, we have to begin by using words. God isn't limited in this way; he very seldom uses words to talk to us. We have the scriptures with the commandments, the inspired teaching of the prophets and apostles, and even the words of the Lord Jesus. Apart from this, God is not likely to address us in so many words, because he wants us to give up "baby talk" and learn to understand his language.

What is the language of God? The Spanish mystic Saint John of the Cross wrote that "silent love" is the language that God understands best. The language that God hears has nothing to do with the sounds we make. God listens to our hearts. He hears our deepest longings and our often unexpressed desires. More than that, God listens to what we do and how we live. God was speaking the language of silent love when he came into this world, born as a tiny baby to a poor young woman in a stable. The Bible tells us that Jesus is the Word of God, the expression of God's care and concern for sinful mankind. God was speaking the language of silent love when Jesus faced suffering and death on the cross.

Learning to speak to God in his language means more than just learning a new set of words or new forms of prayer. It means opening ourselves up to his will and purpose. It means learning to trust him at all times and in all circumstances. It means being totally honest with ourselves and with him about all our faults and weaknesses. It means growing to love him with all our heart and all our mind and all our soul and all our strength – and our neighbour as ourselves.

O God
I used to think it was
all a matter
of learning the techniques,
the language of prayer,
but now I'm beginning
to learn that it's
all a matter
of coming to know
You.

Catalogue Shopping

The most super-organized woman I know is a friend who does all her shopping by mail. She says it saves a tremendous amount of time. All she has to do is pick up her favorite catalogue, decide what she wants and send off for it. No babysitter to pay, no travelling time, no wandering around the stores looking for something that probably isn't there anyway. She even had me sold on the idea at one point. It isn't that I don't like shopping. I love shopping. It was all the complications that wore me down. And the catalogue looked so good!

It wasn't a totally unsuccessful venture. But I did send back more things than I kept, and finally stopped ordering from the catalogue altogether. The problem was that things were seldom the way they looked in the pictures. A soft rosy-red dress turned out be a vivid scarlet. A pair of sheets had a seam running smack down the middle. Some children's mittens were replaced with others "of similar quality or better" – all very well, but not what I had ordered.

Sometimes I think we get into a habit of looking at life from a catalogue point of view. We set our hearts on achieving some particular life-style or measure of affluence, only to discover that it's not all it was cracked up to be.

A few years ago, the hilarious movie *Bedazzled* tried a modern remake of the old Faust legend. A handsome young devil offers to buy the soul of a young man in return for seven wishes. The young man is desperately in love with a girl who won't give him the time of day. He is tongue-tied in her presence, so first of all he wishes to charm her with witty conversation. This succeeds beyond all expectation. But when he tries to kiss her, she screams.

After a few more fumbling attempts, the young man finally gets his wish perfected . . . a little rose-covered cottage, baby in the high chair, himself arriving from work, she greeting him with a passionate kiss, both madly in love with each other. And then her husband walks in.

The point was that the devil always gave a little less than the young man thought he was going to get. He had a picture in his mind, but the reality never lived up to it. Basically this is what the Bible has always taught us about sin. The cost will probably be higher than we expected, and it certainly won't be as good as it looked. On the other hand, God doesn't always give us what we expect either. Like the catalogue store, he reserves the right to substitute with "similar quality or better." Usually it's better.

A common problem among Christians, particularly new Christians, is recognizing God's answers to prayer. Sometimes they don't look like real answers at all. We may send off a catalogue prayer for a new spiritual dress, green with long sleeves. Back comes a bicycle or a new roasting pan. It doesn't make much sense to us, and we wonder if our prayer was ever processed.

Psychologists tell us that the sign of a creative mind is that it doesn't run in the usual channels. It reaches an unexpected conclusion through a series of intuitive jumps, which are then worked out in a logical way. God is utterly creative, and his answers to prayer are creative too. We may think that the answer to prayer A should be B, but instead we get C and D, which look ridiculous if not disastrous. However, this eventually gets us to E which is a far better solution than B would ever have been.

God never gives catalogue answers to our prayers. What suits Mr Jones down the street may not suit us. God knows it, even if we don't. He always wants the best for us and we have to learn to trust him for it.

When our children were little, I always dreaded the pre-Christmas season on the television. The toy advertising was strong and insistent. "Silly Sally is the doll that wiggles and giggles. Make your friends laugh." Or "Peter Pony is the horse you can ride. Be a real cowboy this Christmas!" Children are too immature and inexperienced to withstand the impact of this kind of advertising. They don't know enough about toys to realize that gadgets have a high breakage rate, that batteries need replacing. They don't know enough about money to realize that one Peter Pony might equal a pair of new skates and a toboggan and some books, along with a box game or two. They don't even know themselves well enough to realize that they'll be bored to tears with Peter Pony or Silly Sally only a day or two after Christmas.

Sometimes we're a bit like children too. We eagerly watch all the commercials on the world and then send off our orders like a child writing to Santa Claus. But we don't always know about the problems or the real cost, or even that it isn't what we really want.

Years ago, when my children were little, I remember getting very depressed about the state of my house. All my friends kept immaculate homes with gleaming floors and polished tabletops. When they dropped by my house, I always seemed to be wading through a sinkful of dirty dishes, with toys all over the kitchen floor, and a living room rug that badly needed vacuuming. In desperation I prayed fervently for help in being a better housekeeper.

What I really wanted from that prayer was a little gentle stiffening of the moral fibre. What I got were the plagues of Egypt! Red ants coming through my dining room window, black ants in the bathroom, some mysterious and never-identified green bugs in the kitchen, and moths in the linen closet. All in 48 hours. Needless to say, my house was cleaned out, tidy, and ship-shape in no time. But help like that I can do without!

It was my first experience of God's unique sense of humour. I learned that after some prayers (if you really meant them) you had better duck, that God doesn't help us to do something we are quite capable of doing on our own, and that a lot of other things are more important than being an immaculate housekeeper.

O God
So often I know what I want,
I'm sure of what I need,
I've got a real hunch about
what would be best.
It's taking me a long time
to learn
that I don't really see
the whole picture.
Things will only
fall into place
in my life
and in my prayers
when what I really want
is You.

Being Afraid

Getting out the vacuum used to provoke moments of sheer terror in our house. Our two toddlers would run screaming for the highest point in the living room and there, perched on the back of the living room sofa, they would watch in awed fascination as the awful monster gobbled up the dirt and litter on the rug. No dragon ever had a worse reputation. Only when the machine was safely unplugged and disassembled, would they dare to approach it. Having not yet learned that big things like children will not go into little things like vacuum nozzles, they were understandably nervous of being sucked up too.

The same thing happened at bathtime. The minute the bathtub plug was pulled, there would be a frantic scramble for safety. Nobody wanted to go down the drain. It was a small hole, just two inches across, and no child could possibly have got more than his big toe or a couple of fingers into it. But reassuring words fell on deaf ears. Standing on the bathmat with towels wrapped around them, they would watch the dregs of the water swirl out of the tub and gurgle down the pipe. It was definitely safer to be out of that situation!

Ridiculous as these fears were, they at least had some obvious basis. What gave me far more concern were the irrational fears that seemed to spring from nowhere – pigs under the bed, scarecrows in the cupboard, and "bad guys" in the basement. It didn't make any sense. Bad guys could presumably be traced to television but our children had never seen a pig or a scarecrow.

The worst time came when our two-year-old suddenly developed a terror of ants. He could spot an ant on the sidewalk ten paces away and was quite prepared to leap into the path of an oncoming car rather than step over the tiny insect. This was the same child who would run quite happily to pet strange dogs tied outside the supermarket. Knowing the tendency of Dobermans and German Shepherds to snap at irritating strangers, even baby ones, I often wished that my child's morbid fear of ants could be transformed into a healthy regard for strange dogs and fast cars.

Trying to cope with this infantile phobia one day, while we were eating lunch in the backyard with ants crawling all over the picnic table, it suddenly occurred to me that God must get as frustrated with us as I was with my baby. We too are afraid of the wrong things. We are afraid of poverty and ill health and death. It seems only natural that we should be afraid of these things and that we should do what we can to avoid them. Yet Jesus said, "Take no thought for tomorrow."

Living in poverty himself, with nowhere to lay his head, Jesus advised the rich young ruler to give away his wealth. He healed the sick and raised the dead to life. The deep fears mankind has borne in every age, Jesus showed to be unnecessary. With Jesus' death and resurrection in mind, Saint Paul was able to quote: "O Death, where is your sting? O Grave, where is your victory?" No longer did Christians need to be afraid of poverty or ill health or even the ultimate enemy, death.

The rub is that while Jesus told us not to be afraid of some things, he did not tell us that there was nothing to fear. On the contrary, he said there are some things that ought to give us more than a moment's uneasiness. "Do not fear those who kill the body, but cannot kill the soul. Fear him rather who is able to destroy both body and soul in hell."

There are reasons for being afraid, but we haven't got the right ones. Like little children, we run away from ants and step in front of a fast car. We fear material poverty and ignore the starving spirit. We fear ill health but not the sickness of soul caused by sin. We fear death but not what comes after death. We have learned to love God but not to fear him.

The biblical injunction to fear God tends to raise a lot of questions in the modern Christian community. How can we fear God when we are told to love him? Doesn't perfect love cast out fear? Why should we be afraid when God has so obviously shown how much he loves us? To begin with, the Hebrew word for *fear* in this context carries with it many connotations of reverence and respect. The Lord God of the Universe is neither a chum nor a pal. He is our father and is willing to be a friend, but he also demands our respect.

There is a story told of King George VI of England, who still found time for family fun and games after he undertook the arduous responsibilities of the monarchy. There was much love and affection in the family, but the two little princesses always had to remember that their father was the king. Once Princess Margaret was overcome by excitement and called out in the heat of a game, "Oh, Daddy, don't be a fool!" In the immediate and icy silence which followed, the little girl realized that she had made a serious mistake. No one, not even his own daughter, may call the king of England a fool. If human majesty must be so respected, how much more should we respect the heavenly King?

At a more humble level, parents who demand respect from their children seldom find that this prevents love. On the contrary it appears that children who respect their parents are more likely to love them. The three-year-old who calls his mother names and kicks her on the shins when he doesn't get a candy bar at the store is not learning to love her.

The Bible tells us, at least three times, that the fear of the Lord is the beginning of wisdom. Anyone who would become wise in the ways of God must begin with respect and reverence. Like Moses, taking off his shoes before the burning bush. Like the disciples, awed at the sight of the risen Christ. Like Saul, struck down and blinded on the road to Damascus. Like scores of ordinary men and women since, who have suddenly known the hand of God in their lives and trembled.

My children laugh now when I tell them how they were afraid of going down the bathtub drain. Is it possible they could ever have been so foolish? Didn't I tell them how silly their fears were? Of course I told them, but they didn't believe me. God tells us not to worry about money or sickness or even death, but most of the time we don't believe him.

O God
I used to think
my fears would disappear
when I grew up.
All that's happened
is that my fears have changed.
I know they're foolish,
but didn't I read
in the Bible
that the beginning of wisdom
is the fear
of You.

Waste

One of the more unpleasant household chores, normally delegated to younger members of the family, is taking out the garbage. Admittedly the advent of green plastic bags has helped considerably, but it's amazing how the stench of rotting melon rind and decaying chicken bones manages to escape through the non-porous polyethylene of which the bags are made.

What surprises me even more, however, is the amount of garbage that a family of five can produce – bags and bags of it on occasion. We are not particularly wasteful people. Leftovers are normally recycled into soups. Old clothes go to rummage sales. But still there is the big green bag ready for every collection day.

Christians, it seems to me, have a responsibility for avoiding waste, especially because we live in an age of such over-riding affluence. Sometimes there is so much of everything that it doesn't seem important to conserve what we have. And yet the Bible tells us a different story.

There were two occasions when God took a direct hand in feeding his people. The first time he sent manna for the hungry Israelites in the desert. There was a great abundance of it, more than they could possibly eat. (God never does anything by halves!) But the Israelites were warned to gather only as much as they could eat in a single day. If they gathered more, it rotted and bred worms. Left on the ground, it simply disappeared and more appeared the next day. Here was an important lesson for the Israelites. Greed led to waste. If they exercised restraint, God provided enough for everyone.

The second incident happened when Jesus was followed by a large crowd of people to a remote and lonely place. Having taught them for the better part of the day, the Lord had pity on them because they were hungry. The feeding of the five thousand is the only miracle recorded in all four gospels. It must have made a tremendous impression on the disciples. Here was a great mob of hungry men, and Jesus fed them all with two loaves of bread and five small fishes!

And there were leftovers! I have often been at church suppers and seen what a hungry crowd can do to a table full of casseroles. Usually there isn't a scraping left. Yet here were 5,000 people who were more than ready for their dinner, and Saint John tells us that the disciples took up twelve baskets of scraps. When God provides, he gives in abundance, far more than we ever need. But also, he doesn't want anything wasted. Jesus came to show us what God is like, and he ordered the disciples to gather up all the bits of leftover bread and fish *so that nothing would be wasted.*

Now this says something about our stewardship of the world's resources, but I think it also says something about us. If not a sparrow falls to the ground without God seeing it (and as Jesus said, we are worth more to him than many sparrows), then surely the same Lord who is concerned that not a scrap of bread be wasted will be even more concerned that not one of his children be wasted.

There is so much waste of human potential in our world. Young children are brutalized in the unfeeling street culture of urban ghettos. Teen-agers become alcoholics and dope addicts. Bright young men and women who lack educational opportunity or encouragement get stuck in mind-numbing, routine factory operations. A man in the prime of life is struck down by a fatal heart attack, or a young mother develops cancer. The list seems to be endless, and we wonder what God can do to prevent the emptiness of all this waste.

God does not see as we see, and his ways are not always our ways. Sometimes what we think of as waste is not what he would call waste. When Mary Magdalene poured a bottle of precious ointment on Jesus' feet to show her love for him, Judas Iscariot said it was a terrible waste. Surprisingly Jesus did not agree. He made the cryptic comment that she had anointed his body for burial and that what she had done would be remembered through the ages. God did not look upon this outpouring of Mary's love as a waste.

We must try to look at the problem of waste from God's perspective. How impossible that often is, and yet God has given us standards by which to judge. It concerns the commitment of our lives to his will and purpose.

Obviously child prostitution or teen-age drug rings could never be part of the will of God for a young person's life. As Christians we have a clear responsibility to fight against such evil and prevent it wherever possible. The bright young man who ends up in a factory job because no one ever encouraged him to reach any higher is wasting the intellectual talent God gave him. But what do we say about the Little Brothers of the Poor who have given their lives to God's service and who deliberately choose to work in that same factory situation in order to show the love of God there? Is that also a waste?

When Mother Teresa first went out on the streets of Calcutta to look after the frail old people who were dying there, some critics said it was a waste. Why keep such people alive for a few more hours or days of meaningless existence? But the sisters listened to God and not men. Now the work has expanded to include orphanages and hospitals all over the world. Mother Teresa is recognized as an international heroine. No one any longer would criticize the work she and her sisters are doing, or say that it is a waste. Such is the effect of public acclaim. The same thing is true of Jean Vanier and his work with retarded adults in France. Now *L'Arche* houses have begun to spring up all over the world.

But is it any more important or worthwhile to care for other people's parents or children than it is to care for our own? When a woman leaves a successful career to stay home and look after an aging parent or a retarded child, aren't we inclined to dismiss it as a waste? Don't we say, at least by inference, that this is something anybody can do and she after all has talent and prospects and a great future ahead of her? The trouble is, "anybody" won't do it. If her own daughter isn't concerned, how many other people are going to care about a cranky, confused old woman? And how many people are prepared to take on the extra work of helping a retarded child reach his full potential? There are always plenty of people who are ready to tell us we are wasting our time and talents, but the question we always need to ask ourselves is, Would God say it was a waste? Is this a jar of precious ointment he wants us to offer out of love for him?

I think that in our society being a mother must be the most undervalued work a woman can do. Diapers and dirty dishes are seen as the absolute end-of-the-line. Full-time mothers earn no salary, have no credit rating, pay no income tax, and do not "contribute" to the Gross National Product. At a dinner party, it's considered quite acceptable for doctors to talk about medicine, for teachers to talk about education, for businessmen to talk about growth potential and the state of the economy. But let the mothers in the gathering begin to talk about children, and immediately they are teased into subjection and told to talk about something "interesting."

Women have reacted to this wholesale devaluation of the home by getting out of it. If enough people, newspapers, magazine articles, and television shows tell a young woman that it's a waste of her education and abilities for her to stay at home and look after a couple of snotty-nosed brats, what else can you expect her to do?

When I was a young university graduate, housework was not my idea of a fulfilling vocation. Fortunately it never occurred to me that I could have my children and leave them too. Daycare centres were not yet invested with roseate credentials of "superior care." Everyone took it for granted that day-care centres were where you left a child if you couldn't manage anything better. Whatever the options, a mother's care was always considered to be better than anything else.

It would be untrue to suggest that I went blissfully forward into motherhood without any second thoughts. Sometimes I reflected grimly on the old joke about the mother who wanted her daughter to have a college education "so she'll have something to think about while she's washing the dishes." (The joke has lost its point, and nobody tells it anymore.)

There did come one stage when I thought back over the preceding twenty years and wondered whether I had "wasted" the talents and abilities God had given me. Looking at it from my own particular perspective, it was easy to think that this might be so, and my unhappiness deepened. But when I prayed about it, I realized that God had a very different point of view. I had made a personal commitment to him long before I married or had children. Always before making any major decision in my life, I had tried to seek his will. Thinking back over those twenty years, I couldn't see any point in my life when I should have made a different decision or when my life should have taken a different turning. Never was I called upon to do anything more heroic than to cook and wash and mend and tell bed-time stores. Therefore, *logically,* I had to come to the conclusion that if this was where I was, it was where God wanted me to be. And if it was where God wanted me to be, there could be no waste!

I think that there must be many young mothers who are now experiencing the same feelings of frustration and futility and self-doubt which I have known, and I wish that somehow, through their faith and in their churches, they could find a community of help and support for an unrespected and often difficult vocation. Jesus said that if we would find our life, we must first lose it. Somehow I always had a mental image of casting one's life away in a grand and glorious gesture. It never occurred to me until recently that one could lose it just as well in driving the ballet class car pool or making popcorn on a rainy day.

O God
How often my life
seems a waste
(and sometimes I must admit
I do waste it).
Give me a continuing
sense of vocation.
Give me a vision
that you're working
your purpose out.
Life only has
its meaning
in You.

"They were afraid of going down the bathtub drain" — *Being Afraid*

Home Sewing

The first major sewing project I ever undertook was also the most unnerving. My four-year-old daughter had been invited to be a flower-girl at her godmother's wedding, and she was absolutely thrilled at the prospect. So was I, until the happy bride dropped off at our house a length of expensive velvet, some lining material, and a complicated dress pattern. I was even more staggered when she said, "Don't make any mistakes. That's the end of the bolt, and we can't get any more!"

Disaster was on my doorstep. I'm the type of seamstress who is always having to rip out mistakes. I had never worked with velvet, had never lined a dress, and had certainly never used a pattern with so many pleats and tucks. Friends whom I consulted informed me that velvet doesn't take kindly to errors in judgement. A ripped-out seam will always show.

Too terrified to begin, I debated with my husband whether we could possibly afford the cost of a good dressmaker. Meanwhile the material sat in the cupboard and the wedding day drew closer. I had begun to wonder whether exposing my daughter to chicken pox and mumps was the only way out of my dilemma when a good friend volunteered to come over and help me make the dress. From then on everything was easy. I learned a lot of new sewing techniques, and I also learned something about the value of friendship.

It would probably have been much easier for my friend to take the material home and make the dress herself. What she actually did was more time-consuming. She came and watched over me while I made the dress. Every step of the way she was there, warning, suggesting, advising, but never actually doing it herself. When the dress was complete, I had made it. On the big day, as my little girl tripped down the aisle, I was proud not only of her but of the dress she wore. Never had I thought myself capable of such a creation.

Sometimes I suspect that if we thought deeply about life we would begin to feel very much the way I felt about making that dress. We have only one life, and when that's gone, we're at "the end of the bolt." It's complicated, and the directions aren't always as clear as we would like them to be. And the worst thing is that all our mistakes show.

But no matter how we feel, we can't shut life away in a cupboard and forget about it. The wedding day, the Feast of the Lamb, approaches, and one way or another, we've got to cut into our material and get on with the business of living. Otherwise we may find ourselves in the position of the man in the parable, who was thrown out of the feast because he didn't have a wedding garment.

Jesus is our pattern for living, but he certainly isn't one of those Easy-To-Make patterns you can whip up in an evening. Like many of the Paris *haute couture* fashions, the pattern he gives us looks deceptively simple. "Love God with all your heart, and your neighbour as yourself." There's a hidden curve in that, and seams on the curve are the most difficult to sew.

It would be much easier if we could lay it all out on the table with definite rules and regulations like "no drinking" or "no birth control." If only we could say, I do this and that, and therefore I live a Christian life, I follow the pattern of Christ. Jesus fasted and prayed, and he said that this was the only way to expel certain demons. The Pharisee in the temple gave alms and fasted, prayed twice a day, and thanked God that he was not as other men, but Jesus said his prayer was useless. How do you come to terms with a "living" pattern which is forever changing size and shape and style right in the middle of your cutting-out?

The wonderful thing about Jesus is that he comes to us not only as a pattern, but as the friend who helps us make the wedding garment. It is something that we need to do ourselves. He cannot do it for us, but he can stand beside us as guide and counsellor, warning us of the pitfalls, helping with incomprehensible instructions.

One thing that always surprises me when I tackle a new pattern is the difference between the flat, cut-out pieces on the table and the finished product. The first time I made a jacket, I could not see how the collar and lapels would fit together. The instructions were there, but I couldn't understand how the process worked. In the end I simply followed the instructions, step by step, not trying to look too far ahead. The end result amazed me because, although far from perfect, it did look like a collar. It was only then that I could see how it had taken shape.

It often happens in the Christian life that we cannot see clearly where we are going until we get there. We may know what the ultimate object is but find it difficult to see how this strange shape in the pattern will end up as a cowl neckline or a full sleeve. Pain, loss, and suffering may turn into joy, gain, and glory, but they are also strange shapes in the pattern. When we look at them spread out on the cutting board, it is impossible to see what the final result will be. Only when the instructions are faithfully followed does something of beauty emerge.

One of the advantages to home sewing is that no two dresses need be exactly alike. The gifted seamstress can always add her own touch to the most regimented pattern. It is a far cry from the factory where hundreds of look-alike dresses are turned out in the same fabric, in the same pattern, in the same size. If you happen to be unlucky and hit on a popular dress style, you can meet yourself coming and going on any big city street.

God has never wanted look-alike Christians either. We are all called to be followers or "imitators" of Christ, but that does not mean that we are all expected to fit into a mold or conform to a stereotyped pattern. Every Christian is cut from an "original design," like those fantastically expensive dresses that the very rich buy from their Paris couturiers.

Unfortunately we sometimes refuse to accept that original pattern which God is marking out for us. There are styles in religion just as there are in the world of fashion. One year prayer and fasting will be "in," and a short time later it will be social action. Few of us have the courage to do the unpopular thing even when we think God might want it. It is as if God were designing a beautiful evening gown of lace and chiffon, and we tried to cut it off at the knees because everyone else was wearing tweed suits.

And yet it is the Christian who steps out in the clothing that God has provided who becomes a saint. He or she will never be quite like anyone else because there is found in each saint a unique expression of the love of God. Whatever shape this expression takes, we realize that it has always been a part of being a Christian. In another strange way, it is something very new, because no one ever saw it quite that way before, not before Anthony found solitude in the desert, or Francis embraced the Lady Poverty, or Therese said that little things matter. God has something to tell the world through you and through me, that can only be said through you and through me. If others are to hear his word, it is up to us to be faithful in following the pattern he gives us day by day.

O God
Everybody knows that
a stitch in time is worth nine.
But I seem to be in a hurry
rushing around getting the
nine stitches in,
when all I really needed was your
one.
Slow me down, Lord,
that I may let you get
your stitch in.
Maybe then I'll be
more like the pattern
you have for me,
a pattern I can only make
with You.

Making Bread

Making bread is one of those housewifely arts which is coming back into style. It's amazing how often even busy working mothers find time to make their own rolls for a party. Everything else on the table may be plainly served or prepackaged, but homemade bread is the sign of a woman who is doing something more than just coping.

It took a number of failures before I finally developed the knack of making bread. My first loaves were so heavy and indigestible that it was almost impossible to grate them up for breadcrumbs, let alone persuade my family to eat them. Something was wrong, and I couldn't figure out what.

A friend who was an expert breadmaker told me the real secret was in the kneading. "Put lots of muscle into it," she told me. "You can't settle for a few turns around the bowl. You really have to make an effort." Make an effort I did. Better kneaded bread was probably never set to rise, but it still turned out flat and heavy. Depressed by yet another failure, I was on the point of turning in my apron. Other culinary triumphs faded before this basic inability to make bread.

And then along came another friend with a different piece of advice. "Take it easy," she said. "You can't hurry bread. You have to give it time to rise." That was the answer. My cookbook had said to let the dough rise for three hours, and that's what I had done. Always in a rush, eager to smell and taste the finished product, I had been baking half-risen loaves of bread, unaware that they needed either a warmer place or a longer time to complete the process.

I think that very often we make the same mistake in our spiritual lives. Jesus said that we were to be like the leaven in the lump, like the yeast in a bowl of dough. We forget that yeast can only work quickly in the right conditions. Sometimes we think that energy and effort will make a big difference to the world we live in. We go around stirring things up and making a big fuss, and then wonder why the result of all our labour is so small, or so heavy and flat.

Yeast doesn't grow in the process of kneading. It begins to work when things are quiet and still. Slowly but surely, the mounds of heavy dough begin to rise as the little cells of living yeast grow and multiply. In the same way the Bible tells us that what we do and say is seldom as important as what we are. Unbelieving husbands, says Saint Peter, may be won over *without a word being said* "by observing the chaste and reverent behaviour of their wives."

The right temperature is vitally important to the growth of yeast. It develops best in a warm, draught-free room. High heat will kill it, and cold slows it down. The more yeast there is, the faster it grows. I have learned that if I want bread to rise quickly, I have to use extra yeast and put the dough in my warming oven.

All of this applies to our own personal development as well as to the Christian communities of which we are members. Christians are supposed to grow like yeast, and they need an atmosphere of warmth and compassion if they are to develop quickly. Churches and groups which really care about their members are the ones that grow.

Coldness, friction, and discord are all responsible for slow growth, but they aren't the only causes. Sometimes bread takes a long time to rise because there just isn't enough yeast to do the job as quickly as one would like. Sometimes we find ourselves with a very big lump to leaven. One Christian in a situation can never be as effective as two. Jesus was careful to send his disciples out on their missionary journeys by twos because he knew that one would have a very difficult time indeed.

Yeast has needs of its own too. The dry or compressed yeast we buy in the store today needs to be kept in a cool, dry place until it is used. Nor can it be kept in storage too long without losing its vitality. A more old-fashioned and economical way of raising bread is to keep a bowl of liquid yeast on the go. It's a method that goes back into antiquity, like the custom of keeping a small fire-pot in the days before matches.

Somebody gave me a cup of sourdough starter recently, together with a page of instructions on how to use it and how to look after it. I was too busy at the time to try any new recipes, but I did manage to follow the other instructions. I learned that sourdough should be stirred every day, and that it needs to be "fed" at least once a week. Everything was fine for the first two or three weeks. I remembered to stir and I added the flour, milk, and sugar. Then, what with one thing and another, I forgot. Days went by, and suddenly I realized that my sourdough had not been stirred. More than two weeks had gone by since its last feeding. Quite noticeably, the tiny air bubbles were no longer to be seen in its glass jar. The sourdough was dead, or dying.

Fortunately it could still be revived, and my family is now getting fat on hot biscuits and dumplings. But it made me think about the leaven in the lump. Yeast can't be kept in storage too long and neither can our faith. My sourdough starter needed feeding to keep alive, and so do we. We need a daily stirring up, and we also need the solid weekly nourishment that Sunday brings.

Another thing about yeast is that it only fulfils its purpose when mixed up in the dough and rising. Sometimes we are tempted to draw away from the world. We know we're not supposed to be *of* the world, but sometimes we don't even want to be *in* it. We lock ourselves into Christian ghettos, with Christian friends and church activities, and maybe send our children to Christian schools. All of these are good and have their place, but we have to be careful that they don't take over. The world is not going to come knocking at our door. We have to be willing to go out and be mixed into it. Business, school, volunteer work, social life. They all provide an opportunity to bear a witness, to lighten the load for others, to be the leavening in the lump of humanity.

O God
It seems to take me
a long time to learn
that things work when
they're in the "right" time.
Help me to learn
to live in your time.
Keep me from being flat,
keep me alive and nourished,
that in Jesus I may rise
to You.

Changing Prices

Living in the centre of a large city has, for me at least, one distinct advantage. We may not have much of a garden, but only five minutes away is a large and flourishing farmers' market. Here can be bought varieties of fruits and vegetables which seldom grace the produce shelves of my supermarket. Plum tomatoes, purple broccoli, black currants, raspberries, leeks, broad beans, red potatoes and lettuce – all make their appearance in due season. Ripe and fresh-picked, standing in the shelter of the shaded stalls, the vast profusion of the harvest never fails to astound me.

It might be assumed that bargain prices, in addition to quality and variety, would be an inducement to shop at the market. I found on my first visit that this was not the case. Prices were seldom higher than at the chain stores, but neither were they often much lower. Nor was there competition among the sellers. From one end of a long row to the other, the price of a head of lettuce would be the same. Obviously there had been a certain amount of price fixing. Nobody haggled. Nobody ever tried to bargain, except that sometimes a better price would be offered if you agreed to buy in quantity.

In several years of shopping at the market, I had only one real "buy." I turned up at the market towards the end of a long, hot day and bought twelve baskets of strawberries at about two-thirds the going price. The berries were very ripe (which was why they went cheaply), and I had to put them in the freezer that night. I didn't know at the time how good the price was, or I would have bought more.

Trying to repeat the purchase a few days later, I discovered my mistake. It was no good going back at the end of the afternoon either. By then all the strawberries had been sold with the exception of one stall, where the price was even higher than the one quoted in the morning. There were no more bargains in strawberries.

This simple incident is a good example of the basic economic law of supply and demand. The price of anything almost always depends on how much somebody is willing to pay for it. Eggs may be plentiful, therefore eggs are cheap. But in a time of war or natural disaster, with hunger and famine rattling at the door, eggs become literally worth their weight in gold. Priceless family heirlooms are bartered for a dozen eggs, a few loaves of bread, a pound of cheese.

In more normal times, the same principle can be seen at work in the art market. What makes a Rembrandt worth a million dollars? Why is some strangely shaped blob of metal by a contemporary artist worth even thirty thousand? The answer, of course, is that someone is willing to pay that price.

We have a friend with a valuable collection of paintings by Cornelius Krieghof. Canadian winters of long-ago are shown in snowy landscapes with panting horses, dashing sleighs, habitant farmers in red tuques and sashes. Krieghof's paintings sell for thousands of dollars, but our friend inherited his collection from a grandfather who had lived in Quebec City at the same time as the artist. The grandfather had bought all these paintings at the going price of ten or fifteen dollars, partly because he liked the paintings and partly because he felt sorry for the artist, who had a family to feed and not much money. It doesn't make sense that Krieghof's paintings should have been "worth" only ten or fifteen dollars then, and sell for fifteen thousand now.

In a way, you could say that God is like a master artist who paints beautiful scenes of indescribable beauty and forms living sculptures that move and breathe. What price do we put on all these? How well do we value all that has been put into our care? Like other great artists, God also had a masterpiece. One work of his creation stood out above everything else – this was man himself. Here was a sculpture in living flesh that moved and acted, that thought and loved, and had the possibility of becoming a true child of God.

And what value did man put on man? What price was set on a man's life in Vanity Fair? Now that slavery has been almost eradicated from the world, it seems strange that a man's life could be valued in terms of dollars. It seems strange that someone who has been set "a little lower than the angels" could be sold for silver and gold. And men were worth even less than that when kings and generals sent soldiers into hopeless battles, or landlords turned starving peasants off the land. It seems that the value of a man depends on what the market will bear.

The worst job anyone ever asked me to do was to help on the pricing committee of the church bazaar. It was an unnerving experience. How can you put a realistic price on a gaudy wool afghan, when you know that it has taken someone upward of a hundred hours to knit, that it has at least fifty dollars' worth of materials in it, and that you will only have six hours to sell it?

We had such an afghan. Every bazaar does. We thought surely someone would want this beautiful pink-and-green afghan at a rock-bottom price of sixty-five dollars! It was good value if you worked out what the stores would charge. But the morning passed and nobody bought the afghan. Other members of the committee came along and said it was a ridiculous price and nobody brought that much money to a bazaar anyway. So the price came down to thirty-five dollars because by that time we only had the afternoon period to sell it.

By mid-afternoon the price had slipped to twenty-five dollars, and the afghan still hadn't sold. It lay there on the table, spread out in all its pink-and-green glory, waiting for the right buyer. Just then the woman who had made it arrived and saw the price tag we had pinned to all her hard work. She was furious and complained bitterly to the bazaar committee but they explained that the afghan hadn't sold and asked what else they could do about it. Frustrated and angry, she came back to our table, snapped out twenty-five dollars, and bought the afghan back! It was, she said, a bargain at the price.

In a way, that's what God did with us. Ranked at the top of creation, we valued ourselves too little and had soon sold ourselves into slavery and sin. But God knew how much we were really worth. He knew the work and effort that had gone into our creation. He knew the value of the materials. And like the woman at the bazaar, God bought us back!

There is one big difference though. The woman bought her afghan back at a cheap price. God probably could have done the same thing. He could have bought us at the price we set on ourselves, but he didn't. He set his own value on us, and he paid that price. It was the highest price that could be paid – Himself. Jesus said, "Greater love has no man than this, that a man lay down his life for his friends."

O God
I was overwhelmed
when I first realised
how much you thought
I was worth.
How could you think
I was valuable enough
to give your Son?
Let me never forget
your pricing.
Keep me from
devaluing myself.
May I live my potential,
aware of what I am worth
to You.

The TV Set

Every so often I hear a howl of anguish from the den and rush in to find that the TV set has blinked off at a crucial moment in my son's favorite program. By the time I get there, he is up and fiddling frantically with the knobs and buttons. If he's lucky the picture is restored and all is well. Occasionally I have to point out that there are some little words running across the screen that say, "Do not adjust your set. Studio transmission difficulties." Occasionally I suggest that a storm roaring around outside might be responsible for the poor reception. More rarely I admit that the TV set needs fixing, and we have to call a repairman.

The Bible tells us that when we pray, God hears our prayer. But when we don't see the answers coming through loud and clear, we tend to assume that he isn't answering. This is like saying that a blank TV screen means the network isn't broadcasting. During certain hours of the day, assuming that there are no power failures or studio strikes, the network is always broadcasting. If we don't get a picture, the chances are that there is something wrong with our set.

God is always on the job. He doesn't have studio transmission difficulties, union troubles, or anything else to stop him answering us. He has never been known to put out a sign saying, "Do not adjust yourself. I am not answering prayers today."

When we find that we are not getting a good, clear reception in our prayers, it is a sensible idea to look around and see if there is something else which could be causing the problem. Traditional Christian teaching says we need to look at circumstances around us and at ourselves.

Sometimes TV reception difficulties are caused in my part of the world by a raging blizzard. There isn't much we can do but weather the storm and wait. When the blizzard passes on, the picture will be as clear as ever. The same thing is true of life's storms. There often isn't much we can do about them but wait. All these things pass. And we can be sure that unlike the television picture, God's love is coming through to us as strongly as ever, even though we're not picking it up very clearly.

Another outside cause of reception difficulties may be something as simple as birds on the aerial. These are like the distractions we often get in our prayers. They don't last. They come and go, and they aren't worth bothering about much, unless they start to build a nest in the aerial.

But most of the problems are not caused by outside interference. When reception is poor, it's almost always because of the TV set. And when our prayer life is going badly, the cause is almost always to be found in ourselves. When we're having difficulty in communicating with God, it's a good idea to engage in a little self-examination. Sometimes we're doing something wrong, and we know we're doing something wrong, but we don't want to admit it, even to ourselves. And we certainly don't want to admit it to God because then we would have to stop it.

In his autobiography, Norman Vincent Peale tells about an experience he had as a boy. He had stolen some money from his mother's purse and gone downtown to buy the biggest cigar he could find. Then he walked along the street, puffing away and feeling very much the young man. Suddenly his father appeared farther down the street. Instead of running away, Norman quickly put the cigar behind his back and met his father trying to pretend that all was as usual. To make conversation he asked his father to take the family out to the amusement park on Saturday. His father glared at him. "Never make a petition," he said angrily, "and hold a smoldering disobedience behind your back at the same time!"

When we don't seem to be getting any answers to our prayers, it's a good idea to take stock. Do we have any smoldering disobediences that we are trying to hold behind our backs? The sad fact is that sin can separate us from God. It is the only thing that can separate us from God. Saint Paul wrote that nothing – neither death nor life, neither the present nor the future, neither the world above nor the world below, neither trouble, hardship, persecution, hunger, poverty, or danger – *nothing* can separate us from the love of God in Christ Jesus. Yet sin can separate us from God. It won't stop him from sending out his love to us. It stops us from receiving it.

Sometimes all we need to do is make a minor adjustment. We may be neglecting some little duty, failing in some kindness, or allowing ourselves to get too busy so that we have no time for prayer or quiet. If this is all there is to it, we can say we're sorry, take the necessary steps to put things right, and all will be well. It's a bit like turning the adjustment knobs on the TV set. Sometimes though, we find that we're turning those little knobs too often. The picture is turning over and over. The vertical-hold knob catches it just long enough for us to get comfortable. Then the picture starts turning over again. It's time to call the repairman.

I've heard people say a lot of mean things about TV repairmen. How it's almost impossible to find an honest repairman, or one who knows about different models, particularly the one you happen to possess. And if you do find a good repairman, he's always very expensive. One of the nice things about God's business is that it's a monopoly. He isn't only the network sending out the messages. He also supplies the TV sets, and when something goes wrong he does the repair work. Since he made the sets himself, he knows exactly how to fix them even though every model is different. And the best thing of all is that he has already paid himself for the privilege of doing the work!

The only condition is that we have to open the door and let him in to make the repairs. We have to tell him what the trouble is and ask for his help. And then, although it may sound a little obvious, we have to do what he tells us.

My neighbour once had a repairman come to find out why she wasn't getting good reception on channel 6. He tried this and that, and finally he said there was nothing he could do because of the way the house was built. But he showed her that she would get very good reception if she moved the TV set to another location. This wasn't what she wanted and in the end she decided to leave the set where it was and do without channel 6.

Unfortunately this is what happens to many people when they ask God for help in their prayer life. He tells them what the problem is, and they don't do anything about it. Sometimes they protest, "There couldn't possibly be any connection between my prayer life and *that*!" And sometimes they know and are unwilling to do anything about it, like Saint Augustine who prayed in his youth, "Lord, make me holy . . . but not yet!"

Confession before God of all our faults and failings is the way we open the door. He repairs the breaks and tears in our souls with the healing touch of his love and forgiveness. But then there must also be the willingness to be renewed, to change, even to move to "another location" so that we can stay tuned into him, who is the author of all our joy.

O God
I know your message
is loud and clear,
but sometimes I seem to be
such a poor receiver.
As Jesus said, I hear
but I don't hear.
Help me to listen
to what you are saying to me
about what needs
putting right in my life.
Help me to let you
put it right
so that in my inner eye
I may get the whole picture
of the love that comes
from You.

Broken Bones

Not long ago I had one of those calls from the school that chill the marrow of a mother's bones. It was the gym teacher, and he was sorry to tell me that my son had had an accident. It turned out to be only a broken wrist, and not a bad break at that, but for one tense moment I had been thinking of brain concussion, cracked vertebrae – you name it!

Sitting around in the emergency room at a large city children's hospital is enough to shake your thoughts up for quite a while. There is a constant procession of children, and they all have something wrong with them. Kids being what they are, surgery and orthopedics get most of the emergencies. We are, as the Bible says, fearfully and wonderfully made, and how very fragile!

The treatment for a broken bone, as everyone knows, is to set it and put it in a cast. This is very effective, because it stops all stress and strain while the bone knits, but it's also very awkward. Casts are heavy and bulky. They don't bend, and so movement is impossible. The cast provides a healing environment, but I've never met anybody – adult or child – who wasn't glad to get rid of the white plaster bulk by the end of six or eight weeks.

My son was no exception. His arm was almost useless with its stiff and awkward plaster encumbrance. He needed help to button his shirt or put on a coat, had to do homework with his left hand, and took an enforced leave of absence from the basketball team. It was a blessed relief when he finally got rid of the cast and had a free arm once more.

The episode made me stop and be thankful that God made us the way he did. How wonderful it is to have bones with muscles and flesh to cover them, and not the other way around. It would be dreadful to live like a snail or lobster, permanently encased in a hard shell, like someone wrapped in a series of plaster casts from head to toe.

The hard shell does have the advantage of offering some kind of protection. Helmets, shields, and breastplates have been used by fighting men from the very earliest times for exactly that reason. The use of armour reached a ridiculous extreme when medieval knights began to wear whole suits of heavy steel. Covered from head to toe, they could hardly move and once unseated from their powerful war-horses, they were as helpless as a turtle on its back.

Sometimes I think that the physical side of life has a lot to teach us about the spiritual side. God made us with hard, strong bones to hold up all that flabby flesh. And here we are, soft and tender and vulnerable on the outside, with almost no protection from whatever may want to hurt us.

In the spiritual life also this seems to be the pattern we are intended to follow. Everyone needs to have something strong at the centre of their being. It's an almost indefinable quality, and we may say that someone who lacks this inner hardness has no backbone. It doesn't really mean that he literally lacks the physical vertebrae and skeletal structure, but that some important element in the spiritual life is missing.

In the same way God obviously intends us to be as soft and tender and vulnerable on the spiritual level as we are on the physical. We are meant to be open and loving people, and that means we can be hurt. Just as unprotected flesh can be wounded by knives and rocks and fists, so the open spirit can be torn by the unkind word or deed. It is a difficult position to be in, but it is the way God wants us to be.

Sometimes people try a spiritual imitation of the knights of earlier days, and put on their armour. They have been cut or wounded in some previous battle and are determined never to be hurt again. The armour is heavy and uncomfortable, and very difficult to move about in. But it does stop the slings and arrows of outrageous fortune, or one's wife or boss or whoever is getting to us, from penetrating. The trouble is that nothing else penetrates either. The armour gets in the way of a gentle rain, a caress, or a plea for help. Armour has no feeling. There are no little nerve endings as there are in the tender flesh and in the tender spirit.

Being vulnerable does not mean that we have no protection. It means that we can be hurt. But God has given us the means to prevent that hurt from being too great while still preserving the outward sense of touch. We have the ability to build up an inner armour of strong muscles. God may not have meant us to be like the armoured snail, carrying its protection on its back, but neither did he design us to be like the defenseless garden slug.

Our outer flesh gives us contact with the world around us, our bones give us something firm on which to hang that flesh. Muscles give us the ability both to dodge a blow and to absorb it. Professional boxers spend months before a fight building up an amazing musculature designed to protect them from their opponent's blows. Boxers expect to strike blows themselves, and much of their training is directed toward that effort. But just as much work goes into building a strong wall of abdominal muscle to protect the delicate inner organs. The heavy muscles built up directly under the skin protect the well-developed fighter from the extreme bruising of a severe pommelling.

Spiritually we have the same ability to build up muscles. The virtues of faithfulness, kindness, honesty, and humility do not normally appear in our characters overnight. Usually we have to work at developing them. A story is told of a Desert Father who prayed to God for release from all his temptations. It happened as he requested, and he went to the the abbot, expecting him to rejoice as well. But the response of the wise old man was quite unexpected. "You had better go and pray to the Lord to command some struggle to be stirred up in you," he said, "for the soul is matured only in battles."

Bone, flesh, and muscle. The pattern for our physical life is also the pattern for our spiritual life. Bones are the firmness of faith and what we believe. Flesh is the tender heart and feeling spirit. Muscles are the protection of well-developed virtue.

When God came into the world, he showed us what it is like to be truly vulnerable. He was born to a poor young woman, born in a stable because no one was prepared to make room for him in the inn. Soon after, he became a refugee from persecution, taken by his parents to safety in Egypt. Many years later, when Jesus began his adult ministry, the friends and neighbours who knew him best said that he had gone mad, and even his mother and brothers came to take him home. At the end, when his life was in obvious danger, one of his best friends betrayed him.

And yet, when Jesus died on the cross, he was not a broken man. Only his body was broken. His spirit was triumphant. In the midst of all his suffering on the cross, he was able to feel for the sadness of his mother and the disciples. He was able to comfort the penitent thief dying beside him.

Jesus never wavered from a firm belief in the loving purpose of his Father, and his faith remained as strong as bone. The long habit of instant obedience to his Father's will served as the muscle which took him through the agony of his passion to death. Bone, muscle, and flesh. We too are called to be firm, to be strong, and to love.

O God
You know I don't want to be hurt
so it's not surprising
I sometimes think
that if I save my life
I will not lose it,
but Jesus said that
he who loses his life
will save it.
Enable me
to develop that inner strength
which comes from your Spirit
that I may dare
to be vulnerable.
Only then will I
love people
and find the richness of life
that we were meant to have
in You.

Holy Housework

The frustrating thing about housework is the way it has of coming back at you. Mop the kitchen floor and within a few hours it may look as though it hasn't even been swept for days. Give the living room your best spring cleaning and inside 24 hours there will be the tell-tale signs of seeping dust, of lint and litter. Cookie crumbs, dog hairs, unidentifiable bits of paper, and dried mud from somebody's jogging shoes appear almost as if by magic. It's downright discouraging.

Sin, I find, is just like dirt. It's persistent, insidious, and always coming back at me. I confess my failures, ask God for forgiveness, and almost before I can turn around, I fall back into the same old traps of greed and pride, of anger and resentment. I don't know why this should be so surprising to me. It is utterly reasonable that we should act like the dust, since we are made of it. And yet I am always shocked to find myself back in the same old rut, just as I am always shocked to walk into the bathroom I cleaned earlier in the day, before everybody came in from the baseball game and the garden.

Housework has never been my strong point. Whatever improvement there has been over the years has come from watching my tidy friends to see how they manage so easily. They all seem to have a number of habits in common which add up to really good housekeeping, the kind of thing you read articles about in magazines.

They clean up as they go. Watch a tidy housekeeper and you'll see that she doesn't put a spice jar down on the counter and leave it there. She puts it away. The stove is cleaned while she cooks. A wipe here, a wipe there. (It was never very dirty in the first place.)

The same thing is true about sin. It's a lot easier if we clean up as we go. In fact, it is one of the most important spiritual rules. Never let the sun go down on your anger, wrote St. Paul. We may get angry, and sometimes with reason. The important thing is not to brood about it, not to build it up, not to nurse it. Jesus said that if someone sued us, we should come to terms with him promptly, while we were both on the way to court. It is good business advice to settle out of court while you can, but how often we fail to take it as spiritual advice. Resentment, anger, and greed build up until we soon find ourselves in a prison of our own making.

Once I spilled some orange juice in front of the refrigerator. Things were absolutely hectic in the kitchen at that point, so I didn't stop and wipe it up. I simply stepped around it. Unfortunately other people weren't as careful, and the original spill had soon spread its stickiness over an area three times the original spill. Not only that, but by the time the children went to bed, the sticky spots had turned black with dirt and crumbs all ground into it. The whole floor had to be washed before I went to bed, and all for not wiping up one little spill.

We forget that our sin involves other people. We think we can leave it alone and step around it. Before we know what's happened, our family and friends are involved in our anger or resentment. They step in it and spread it around until the mess is almost too big to be cleaned up at all.

They throw out junk. There are a lot of things in my house that I don't need and will never use. Broken garden chairs, single socks, old skis, last week's papers, the list is endless. Tidy housekeepers don't tolerate that kind of mess. They give what they can to a rummage sale and throw the rest out.

Similarly, there are a lot of things in our lives which come under the heading of "spiritual junk." In themselves they aren't harmful or wrong or particularly sinful. But they don't do us any good. I hate to think of the hours I've wasted watching useless TV shows, playing bridge, and going to pointless meetings or parties. We all have our own particular types of junk. One woman may see the neighbourhood coffee party as an opportunity to befriend a lonely young mother, while another woman finds it a real temptation to indulge in gossip. That's why you can't say that any of these things are wrong. In themselves cards or TV or parties aren't wrong, but they can have the same effect that junk has in any other setting.

They live with tidy people. This may sound a little obvious, but good housekeepers always seem to have tidy families. Their children would never dream of leaving coats on the hall closet floor, schoolbooks on the kitchen table, or baseball mitts in the bathroom. I suspect that their husbands also hang up their pajamas and never leave piles of "important" papers on the coffee table in the living room.

Anyway, as I go about picking up the oddments that different members of the family have left here and there, it occurs to me that a lot of the spiritual debris in our lives is caused by other people's problems. It is obviously a lot easier to live a good, Christian life if you live with good, Christian people. A woman who has an adulterous husband, spiteful in-laws, or alcoholic friends can't help but pick up a lot of flack that affects her too.

It may not always be possible to live with spiritually "tidy" people. I'm not sure that God intends us to be insulated in that way. But it is frightening to realize how often wives drink too much because their husbands do, how often teen-agers experiment with drugs because their friends do, how often men cheat on business deals because "everybody does it!" If we are not to be overwhelmed by the world we live in, we all need the strength and support that Christian fellowship can give, in our family if possible and also in the wider church community.

O God
For a minute I thought
I had life under control,
but that bad habit
is back again.
Yet life's victories
are not like the items on a shopping list,
easily ticked off once you've got them.
Lord, it's a struggle
all the way through,
every day.
Keep me struggling, Lord,
so that I may win the victory
in You.

The Country Cottage

One of the things we always wanted (and never had the money to buy) was a country cottage. Within easy striking distance lies some of the most beautiful lake and mountain country in North America, and we've often felt a touch of envy as we watched neighbours packing to go away for the weekend.

But something tells us that it's now or never if we want to have our own cottage. Experts on population trends are forecasting an enormous boom in vacation home sales over the next two decades. More and more young couples are living in apartments with no plans to move into a city house. Instead they are sinking all their available cash into a country home they can use on the weekends and during the summer.

One way and another, we have been lucky about holidays. Sometimes we rented a cottage, or else we borrowed one. Either way the cottage always belonged to someone else. In the process we learned that the way people furnish a country cottage has a good deal to do with how much time they expect to spend there. The most uncomfortable cottage we ever stayed in had never been lived in by the owner at all. He only rented it as a source of income. The beds were lumpy, the chairs were hard, and we always seemed to be running out of cutlery.

By contrast, the most adequate cottage we ever found had been the owner's retirement home until her husband's death a few years earlier. Not only was there plenty of cutlery, but there were all kinds of extra little gadgets that make cooking easier, like a curved grapefruit knife and an automatic toaster that worked. The bedrooms were supplied with extra blankets and shelves of paperback novels, and in one cupboard we found a bonanza of folding garden chairs, a croquet game, and sun-hats!

Building a country home for retirement seems to be gaining popularity. We had one friend who did this and insisted on good construction from the ground up, because he wanted it to be "just right." Only the best materials went into the house, and when he got appliances, they were new expensive ones, because he expected to be living there permanently.

In one sense, this is the way we ought to be preparing for heaven. It's a "retirement" of sorts, at least from this life, and we ought to consider how we are going to spend it. Jesus said he was going to prepare a place for us, but what if he has to build with the materials we provide? The best carpenter in the world can do little with green lumber, crooked nails, and insecure foundations.

The good works and kind actions we do on earth may not show any tangible result in this life, but in heaven they may be the difference between a mansion and a shack. Someone like Mother Teresa working among the poor and outcast, may have few of this world's goods. Like the young families living in small city apartments, she has put everything she has into a "country home."

Jesus told us to lay up for ourselves "treasure in heaven," where we wouldn't have to worry about moths and rust and theft. There are no taxes to pay on a cottage in heaven and no high insurance rates against fire and vandalism. There isn't even any problem with inflation. Cottages there don't cost any more than they ever did. Or perhaps I should say that the price is as high as it ever was – yourself.

Owning a country cottage isn't high on everybody's list of priorities. Some people only drive out to the country once in a while, just to make sure it's still there. To people like this, moving to the country on a permanent basis would be sheer misery. They would be bored and lonely and always longing for the bustle of city life.

Few people would think of moving to the country after retirement unless they had tried living there on a short-term holiday basis to see if they liked it. On the other hand, all kinds of people seem to assume they will love being in their heavenly cottage even though they aren't too sure what the countryside will be like.

C.S. Lewis wrote about people like this in *The Great Divorce.* He described hell as a grimy, half-deserted town whose self-centred and quarrelsome inhabitants were perfectly free to get on a bus and go to heaven any day they liked. Those who made the day's excursion were invited to stay and not go back to hell at all! The problem was that heaven didn't really suit them. The light was too bright, the grass hurt their feet, and everything was somehow too *real.* Tragically, at the end of the visit, all but one of the tourists decided to go back to the private hell each had created for himself.

The Holy Spirit, writes Saint Paul, is a "foretaste" of heaven, a guarantee of what we're getting. We can't stay in heaven on a permanent basis, but we can have glimpses, we can pay visits, we can even have little holidays. God isn't trying to pull a fast one. He isn't trying to sell us some undrained swamp or blasted desert. He wants us to see for ourselves.

Promoters of retirement villages in Florida and Arizona occasionally offer free trips to people interested in visiting the site and seeing the amenities. That's what God does for us. The experience of conversion, a weekend retreat or a "sweet" hour of prayer, the strange warming of the heart, all give us a strong impression of the true joys of heaven.

The best thing about our heavenly cottage is that we can get to know "the neighbours" before we even move. In fact, God is quite prepared to come and visit with us in our city home if we only ask him. He wants to be the best friend we ever had.

People who plan to retire in the country usually do what they can to make things comfortable before they go there. While they are working, they still have a good income and can afford to make improvements. Nobody knows if heaven is really a place of complete retirement and rest, but the indications are that these are our prime earning years. It's quite possible that the changes we don't make now may never be made. Eternity is a long time to spend with lumpy beds and no bath-tub!

O God
Saint Paul says you meant
me to be
a temple of the Holy Spirit.
But at times
I feel more like
a broken down shack.
Yet I know
I must let you be
the Builder,
so that this house of mine
may be a fit dwelling place
in the Spirit
for You.

Board Games

One of our favorite family occupations on a rainy Saturday has been to dig out the Monopoly game and spend the afternoon buying and trading. When our children were young, we used to play Snakes-and-Ladders. As they grew older, we dabbled in slightly more strategic games like Risk and Clue. At one point I thought we must have played almost every board game that had ever turned up on the market.

There are varying degrees of ability required in all these games, but by and large they all depend on the major ingredient of chance. A roll of the dice decides whether you get Boardwalk and Park Place, and the keen Monopoly player soon learns that the owner of these two high-income properties has a distinct edge in winning the game. You can be as astute a landlord as ever walked the streets of New York, but you'll never win the game if your piece keeps landing on Community Chest or Jail while other players are scooping up the prize properties.

Sometimes people look at life as if it were some kind of board game. Chance seems to determine whether or not you are born into a wealthy family, or whether you get a good education. It's chance again that leaves you paralysed after a near-fatal car accident or that puts you in hospital with cancer at the age of thirty. Anything that happens for good or ill, without our own planning, is seen as chance.

But Christians don't look at life as a series of chances. We say that God has a plan for our lives and that somehow all these incidental happenings, which we tend to think of as just "chance," are really part of his over-riding master plan.

It really is amazing sometimes how a "chance" meeting with someone can touch off a series of incidents which profoundly change our lives. Looking back we can see a pattern in the events which was not obvious at the time, and as occasions like this multiply, we become ever more aware of the activity of God behind the scenes. Increasingly, we become sure that there are no chances in life, that God really does have the controlling hand, even in what looks like disaster.

The other side of that picture is that if God has a plan for our lives, why isn't it a little bit clearer? Why are things left to look as if they were happening by chance, and why should God's plan be such a hidden affair?

I think one reason for this is that God doesn't have just one plan. The Bible doesn't talk much about God having a plan; it talks far more about God having a purpose. He wants to win us, as many of us as possible, to himself. On the other hand, he has given us free will, and therefore he has to be ready at any time for us to fall back or change direction or just sit down.

If God had only one plan for my life, it would make no allowance for my inevitable sinfulness. Jesus was the only man who ever completely fulfilled God's plan for his life. With the rest of us, God has to be ready to feint and parry and thrust. He wants to bring us home to himself, and God knows better than anybody else that there is more than one way to achieve his purpose. Whether he accomplishes our final salvation in one way or another is not important to him. The plan always gives way to the purpose.

My teen-age son has recently taken up chess, and in order to sharpen his developing skills, he is prepared to play with anybody who will take him on, including his mother. It is a fascinating game because there are no chances. It is one player against another. The pieces behave in very different ways: rooks move vertically or horizontally, bishops diagonally, knights one square up and two across, pawns move one forward, kings one in any direction, and queens can go as far as they like, any way they like, as long as it's straight. The object of the game is to checkmate the opposing king, which means getting that piece into a position where he can be taken and yet cannot move anywhere else without being taken there too.

Chess is a very intellectual game, and there are a lot of books about it which go into great detail about useful moves. There are snappy plans for winning a chess game quickly, and these are particularly useful if your opponent doesn't know what he is doing. But woe betide the player who goes into a game with just one plan! While he is busy setting up the ideal situation, his opponent will have checkmated his king.

A good chess player needs to have dozens of different plans in his head, and he must be prepared to drop any one of them at a moment's notice in order to develop a different strategy.

It may not be biblical to think of God as a master chess player, but nevertheless I think it's a fair analogy. God wants to bring us to checkmate. He wants to put us in a position where we cannot move without him being able to take us. In the real game of chess, the king is never taken. He is only put in the position where he can be taken and must concede defeat. It is the same with us. God does not take us against our will, but he is prepared to put us in a position where we could be taken, where the only reasonable thing to do is give up and own him as Lord and Master.

In order to get us into that position, God will use all the resources he has. My valuable queen may be taken by an overlooked pawn, and a forgotten knight will stalk my remaining bishop. And if God has to strip his own side of the board as well as mine in order to put me in checkmate, he will do it. But suppose we want to be taken? Suppose we are prepared to own God as master of our lives – what then? We find ourselves playing more and more on his side of the board. There are so many others that he wants to bring to himself, and we can help.

The important reason for remembering that God has a purpose for our lives, and not just a plan, is that it is never too late for us to fulfill that purpose. The time for a particular plan may come and go. How often do we all lament the lost opportunities, the things that we should have done and failed to do?

Saint Augustine knew this feeling as well as anyone. After living a dissolute life in Rome, struggling to escape from the God who pursued him, he was finally won over. Only then did he realize how much he had missed by saying no to God for so many years. "Too late am I come to love Thee, O thou Beauty, so ancient and withal so new," he wrote in his famous *Confessions.* "Too late am I come to love Thee."

Looking back over Augustine's life, we can see from our own vantage point that it was far from being "too late" for God's purpose. The very things which had contributed to Augustine's sinful state now became positive advantages on God's side of the battle. The innocent Augustine, converted in his youth, might never have become the great doctor of the church without the philosophical training he received in the pagan universities of Rome. God certainly did not plan for Augustine to lead a life of immorality, and undoubtedly there were earlier plans which would have served his purpose equally well. The point is that when Augustine finally did turn to God, it was not too late.

It is never too late for us to find God's purpose in our lives, as long as we still draw breath. *The Shorter Catechism* puts it very succinctly: "The chief end of man is to glorify God and enjoy him forever." Even the penitent thief on the cross was able to come into that state of grace.

O God
Sometimes they call it
the "game of life,"
but you know
and I know
that it's for real.
So often reality eludes me
as I made my false moves
to cover up my mistakes.
Let me begin again
to discover your rules
so that in the struggles of life
I start winning the victory
in You.

Being Fair

No matter how large or small the family, there is one inevitable result of parental discipline: the oldest child always complains that the youngest is getting away with murder. And a lot of the time, he's perfectly justified in his protests. Inexperienced parents tend to be a lot stricter with their first-born simply because they don't know how easy-going they can afford to be. The most elementary common sense tells us that it is far easier to slacken the rules later than it is to tighten things up once you discover you haven't been strict enough!

A secondary effect of being strict with the first-born is that he then automatically keeps the younger members of the family in line. If the oldest child wasn't allowed to cross Main Street until he was six years old, he's not going to let his little brother do it at five. And if an unwary five-year-old should try it, Big Brother is sure to find out and report the matter to the authorities.

Children want things to be fair. They desperately want life's prizes to be evenly distributed so that no one child gets more than another. When dessert time rolls around, as any harried mother can testify, it's uncanny how even the sloppiest child can gauge precisely which piece of cake is fractionally larger than the others! It's not that he would object to eating the larger piece of cake. He just doesn't want anybody else to have it.

The trouble is that life isn't fair. It would be so much easier for parents if everything could be divided up evenly. But every child is born with his own innate advantages and problems. Some children are clever; others have learning disabilities. Some can't see or hear properly, and others turn out to be natural athletes. Even at the level of personality, it is amazing how quickly character differences show up in the tiniest baby. Some are quick tempered, some are persistent, some are impatient, and others are very relaxed. And then, some children are born into happy, secure families while others grow up in an atmosphere of discord and hate. Life is not "fair" in the sense that our children interpret it.

When it comes to a matter of discipline and meting out punishment, parents soon realize that a fair reprimand for one child may be too harsh for another. A spanking may leave one little boy in perfectly good spirits, while another child is crushed by a cross word. This is one of the reasons why it is so difficult to make hard and fast rules about disciplining children. Some need more strictness, while others grow and develop better in a flexible atmosphere.

God has the same problems with us. We want him to be "fair", and most of the time we refuse to recognize that a wise and truly loving father will treat all his children according to their own needs and abilities. The child who wasn't allowed to cross Main Street until he was six will object if his little brother is allowed to cross by himself at the age of five, and there is no way his parents could make him understand that his little brother is considerably less impulsive than he was, and much more ready to pay attention to turning cars and red lights. The parents can see this, but the big brother is too involved in the situation. He thinks his parents are playing favorites.

Our heavenly Father does not play favorites, but he does treat us all differently. God knows us as no one else can ever know us. He who made us is aware of every need, every desire, every frustration. He also knows our abilities and what we are capable of doing. Jesus said that when someone had been given a great deal, much would be expected of him. The more talents we have, the greater is our responsibility to use them well.

As a parent I found that one of the most difficult things to cope with was tale-bearing. There were family rules, and I expected them to be obeyed. But sometimes there were valid reasons for overlooking them. One reason is that you can't be down on somebody all the time. Some children have more trouble keeping the rules than others do, and when this happens, the sensible mother makes allowances. Since some rules are obviously more important than others, the trick is to convey to the child in question which rules absolutely must be kept and which rules are flexible. For instance, the rule about not hitting your brother is flexible (he can be very provoking), but the rule about not hitting him with a hammer is absolute. If a difficult child can be brought to obey all the important rules, you're making progress.

The trouble comes when the difficult child has obedient siblings. They almost always do what they're told and they don't really see why the family should have what looks like a double standard. They come in to report the minor transgressions of an erring brother or sister, and then they expect action! Johnny has done something he ought not to have done, and what am I, his mother, going to do about it? It would be so much easier to bring up a family if all the children minded their own business.

God has the same problem with us. Jesus tells Peter he will die a martyr's death, and Peter immediately points to John and says, "What about him?" Martha is busy cooking the Lord's dinner, a necessary and undoubtedly appreciated activity, but she spoils it all by saying, "Tell my sister to come and help." It is to God's credit that he firmly resists all the pressures we bring to bear on him for equality and fairness. What kind of love could he show us if we all had exactly the same abilities and the same gifts?

When our children were young, we always brought each of them a present when we went away on a conference or trip. It was difficult being fair in our choices because we didn't want to buy one child a very expensive gift without getting an equally valuable gift for the others. Sometimes a certain toy would be just right for a particular child but there was nothing in a similar price range or quality for the other two. We could see that they would be quite happy with less expensive toys, except that they might be aware that one toy of the three was more costly. And since this in itself would cause problems, we usually got them all inexpensive toys without satisfying the one child who really would have appreciated the more expensive gift.

Once however, I made a much worse mistake than that. I found a savings bank, a delightful affair made of clear plastic which automatically sorted in full view all the coins that were put into it. It seemed to me that any one of my three children would be tickled with that bank, and since I could not decide who would be the favored recipient, I ended up by buying three of them, one for each child.

It really wasn't a very successful experiment. Yes, they were pleased with their banks. Yes, they used them and watched the coins sort into the different slots. But somehow the sparkle of real delight was missing. The banks were *all the same,* and I realized later that somehow that present lacked a personal touch.

However much we may complain about God's dealings with his children, we cannot say that he treats us all the same. His relationship with us is on a purely one-to-one basis. No comparisons are allowed. No "fairness" in our human sense is even in the picture. In a typical paradox situation, God loves and treats each one of us as an only child . . . in a very large family.

O God
Comparing could be the death of me.
At least it makes my life miserable
when I'm always comparing what I have
with others.
Even when I talk about "being fair,"
that's just an acceptable way
of standing up for my rights.
But you have a different
standard of fairness
that has nothing to do with comparing
one with another.
Your fairness
is your fatherly concern
for me.
And only when I realize that,
shall I be truly happy
in You.

The Charge Account

There is a lot written these days about generation gaps and cultural barriers, but for downright frustration, I don't think there is anything like trying to communicate with a computer.

Every so often the bills come in and my husband says, "What did you buy from Schnicklehover's that cost $59.78?" I rack my brains for a minute and say, "Nothing that I can think of." He shows me the statement, and if I'm lucky, I can point out that Schnicklehover's is in Ottawa and I haven't been anywhere near Ottawa for the last two years. Otherwise he has to take my word for it, and the statement goes back with everything paid but the $59.78, with a little note explaining that bill isn't ours.

Sometimes that's all we need to do and the matter is cleared up. At other times the Schnicklehover bill will stay on our statement, month after stubborn month. More rarely we may discover that we have received credit for the $59.78!

I suspect that a lot of people look at life as if they had a charge account with God. It's a matter of balanced, regular payments. They live good, clean, and honest lives, and they expect a fair deal from life in return. Then some misfortune or tragedy brings them up short. They say, "What did I do to deserve this?" They feel they're being made to pay for something they didn't do. The way we'd feel if a store wanted us to pay for something we didn't buy. We'd fire off letters of complaint, make phone calls, and tell our friends that we'd never shop at that store again. People treat God like that.

Sometimes, of course, they get credit. Things go really well for them and life seems to have everything to offer. But you don't catch them saying, "Lord, you know I don't deserve all this. You'd better take it back."

When they first came into use, computers were supposed to be infallible. We knew they were going to eliminate a lot of human error, but we didn't know they were going to introduce a lot of computer error. We didn't know that there would still be mistakes on our monthly statements and that they could be harder to trace and pin down than ever before. Computers are not infallible, but God by definition is infallible. If he made mistakes, he wouldn't be God.

God doesn't make mistakes. When things go wrong, when one thing seems to pile on top of another, Christians have always worked from two major premises.

The first is that God in his infinite wisdom, and for reasons that we can't understand, has allowed this misfortune to come upon us. This doesn't mean that he is responsible for it. It means simply that he has allowed it. Jesus said that the hairs of our head are numbered. Therefore when troubles beset us, we have to accept that God is allowing them, just as he allowed men to put Jesus to death on a cross.

The second premise is that if we will put our trust in God during our time of trouble, he will make things come right again. Whatever our hurt, he will heal it. Whatever our sorrow, he will bring us joy. It takes a while to accept this, but it does happen.

Apart from the fact that they sometimes make perfectly outrageous mistakes, computers have another major drawback. They are terribly impersonal. They don't have any heart. A computer may be able to do the billing about 50 times faster than Miss Jones in the accounting department, but it's not nearly so helpful when you have a problem. A computer can solve incredibly complicated mathematical equations in a matter of minutes, when it would take a team of skilled mathematicians several days. It may want to make a note of your name, your age, and your address, but it doesn't care if you like fishing, or that you may be having trouble with your teen-age son, or that your doctor has just said you need a serious operation.

Computers don't care about us as people, as individuals, and for that reason they have become almost the symbol of a depersonalized society. Do not staple, spindle, fold, or mutilate. It's very difficult to talk to a computer. Perhaps for this reason, the message of

Christianity should have a stronger impact on our present world than ever before. It's amazing to think that God who is all-powerful, all-wise, all-everything, should love us and care about us, that he should know our names and our secret longings, and that he should want to come into our lives and share them. It's amazing that he should want to talk with us, that he should really want to communicate with us, that he should want to share in our lives, and that he should want to share some of his life with us.

O God
I've got a bulging wallet
of little cards.
I'm always afraid of losing it because
it's amazing what they will do.
But the more important the little cards become,
the less valued seem to be
my face and my word.
The little cards mean nothing to you,
so I, my face, my word, my life,
mean all that much more
in your sight.
It's because of your great love
that I do have a credit rating,
one I cannot lose
with You.

"God wants to bring us to checkmate" — *Board Games.*

Being Prepared

Every so often I get steamed up by one of those magazine articles about having an "emergency shelf" full of wonderful ingredients that can be transformed into Cordon Bleu casseroles the moment one's husband walks through the door with unexpected company. It always sounds like such a superb idea if only one could be sure of finding the recipe for the said casserole at the same critical moment.

The rather superior alternative of having casseroles at the ready in the freezer suits my lifestyle better, although both methods share the same drawback. Call it Marcia's Law, but the unexpected company always arrives just after I've used the canned crabmeat or the frozen coq au vin for a lesser family emergency and before I've gotten around to replacing it.

Basically, after twenty years of marriage, I've given up trying to convince anyone, including myself, that I'm the world's premiere hostess. If unexpected visitors come, they have to take what they can get. Meat loaf stretches. So does stew. And if we're unlucky enough to be having pork chops for dinner, somebody has to eat fish sticks or cold ham. What is really important, I've decided, is to make sure the guest knows he's welcome and that short rations are a small price to pay for the pleasure of his company. Being prepared for unexpected visitors has a lot more to do with our state of mind than the state of a pantry shelf.

Jesus talked a lot about being prepared and about people who weren't prepared. He spoke about ten foolish virgins who hadn't brought enough oil for their lamps and about an unwise man who built his house on sand. Anticipating the possibility of a late bridegroom or a disastrous flood obviously has important spiritual connotations.

Years ago, when I was a teen-ager preparing for confirmation, our dear old-fashioned minister spent a lot of time teaching us the importance of being prepared for worship. For the most part, this consisted of a good, searching examination of one's conscience and then asking God's forgiveness for any wrong-doing or neglected duties. This was excellent, and it remains the basic preparation for meeting God under any circumstances. The trouble is that too often we assume that the only place we're going to meet him is in church on Sunday.

This was the basic problem of the priest and the levite who "passed by on the other side" when they saw the man who had been beaten up on the way to Jericho. They were prepared to meet God in the temple, and current religious practice decreed that they would unfit themselves for worship if they touched a dead, or even bloody, man.

God always seems to take us by surprise. The whole Jewish nation was expecting the Messiah, but hardly anyone recognized Jesus. And at the final judgement, Jesus warned, we will be surprised to discover that the cup of cold water, or the outstretched hand given to one in need, was really given to him. We must be prepared to meet him wherever we go.

The other side of the coin is that God is also prepared to meet us wherever we are. There is no place in earth or heaven where he is not waiting to receive us. No matter how deep the sorrows we need to pass through or how difficult the way, God is there before us. As for heaven, Jesus said, "In my father's house are many mansions. I go to prepare a place for you."

At a more earthbound level, there is a very practical side to the way in which God is prepared for us. He has prepared things for us to do. In his letter to the Ephesians, Saint Paul wrote that we are created for "good works, which God has already prepared for us to walk in."

When my children were little, they liked to make cookies. What this actually meant was that I mixed up the cookie dough, and they put it out on the cookie pans and baked it. Then they could tell all their friends, over an afternoon snack, that they had made the cookies. The preparation involved was over half the work, but somehow that didn't count. They liked to think that I had nothing to do with it.

Children aren't the only ones who do this. We all tend to forget how much preparation has gone into the things we take credit for doing. I once knit a sweater, but someone else raised the sheep, and sheared, carded, dyed and spun the wool before I began work with my knitting needles. It had all been prepared for me to do, yet my friends are told, "I made the sweater."

There used to be great jokes about women who depended on a can-opener for their culinary achievements. And then there was the famous cartoon about the woman who had "defrosted the dinner all by myself." Now that we live in an era of convenience foods, nobody bothers to laugh anymore. The very fact that stores sell frozen pastry and tinned chopped mushrooms already prepared for use makes it possible for the ordinary housewife to serve her company gastronomic treats like Beef Wellington.

The great rise of do-it-yourself projects during the last 30 years owes a lot to the same principles of prepared work. The home handyman can buy detailed plans and boards sawn to the right length with holes already drilled for pre-selected screws. In the same way, God has already prepared the work he wants us to do. The woman he wants us to comfort may turn out to be our next-door neighbour. The man he wants to receive our witness may work at the next desk in our office or at the gas station where we fill up.

When Mother Teresa of Calcutta decided to go out into the streets of the city to care for the poor and the dying, she did not know where she would find support for the work. But by the end of the first year, she could see how well God had prepared the way. The first members of her fledgling community were the very same school-girls she had been teaching before she went out on the streets. And it was their parents who supplied the first financial support.

When God prepares work for us to do, it doesn't mean that we can sit back and take it easy. It simply means that the work he gives us will be within our capabilities, because he has already done the things which were too hard for us.

O God
Some people are always ready,
but I'm not.
You know that I'm an expert in
the last minute rush
and the short cuts.
I wish I weren't that way,
but that's me.
Yet I want to be prepared in an ultimate sense,
to be open to see you in the things of today,
to not put off till tomorrow
the things you've given me to do today,
and so to live today
that if death should come tomorrow
I may be found in paradise
with You.

Servants

I guess any woman's idea of real luxury is a maid, somebody to do the dirty work and pick up after the family and maybe look after the cooking and dishwashing. I think that would suit me fine, because then I could get on with the really interesting things in life.

There was a time when most middle-class families had at least one maid, and sometimes two. Historians are quick to point out that the mistress of the house still had a lot of work to do, because there weren't all those wonderful electric labour-saving devices then, but I don't believe it. I suspect that my grandmother didn't worry as much about spotless carpets and shiny floors as the TV ads suggest I should, and that her family also wore their clothes a lot longer between washings.

Nowadays only the very rich can afford to have servants, and even they are having trouble, I understand, because nobody wants to do the job at any price. It isn't just the money, because often a cleaning lady makes at least the minimum wage. It seems to be a matter of status. Nobody wants to be a servant. It's demeaning, unless you happen to work for somebody like the Queen or the President. For everybody else, the watchword is equality. Even secretaries these days are telling the boss to go for his own cup of coffee! After all, they aren't servants.

As a result of this late twentieth-century conditioning, I found myself profoundly shocked to realize that being a servant is an essential part of being a Christian. Nobody ever told me that, or perhaps I just never wanted to hear it. If anyone had asked me, I would have said that *freedom* was one of the key words in the New Testament.

After all, there was "the glorious freedom of the sons of God." No longer were we to be slaves, but free. Then somebody asked me to do a Bible study on the word *freedom.*

According to my concordance, *freedom* (or *liberty*) appears in the New Testament a total of 14 times. Only once is it mentioned in the gospels, when Jesus uses a direct quotation from Isaiah to explain his ministry. By contrast, the word *servant* or *slave* (same word in the Greek) appears at least 129 times, and most frequently in the gospels, as Jesus explains again and again the relationships which we are to have with God, with Jesus himself, and with each other. Even the word *serve* appears 27 times. Jesus said,

> "He that is greatest among you shall be your servant."
> "Where I am, there shall also be my servant."
> "Blessed are those servants whom the master finds awake when he comes."
> "The son of man came not to be served but to serve."

Now I know that Jesus told his disciples that he was calling them "not servants, but friends," but somehow one can't get over the suspicion that he felt he had a perfect right to call them servants. No matter how you dress it up, being obedient and "doing the will of the Father" boil down to being a servant. Servanthood is the natural state of the Christian.

It's acceptable enough if you think in terms of being God's servant. That is a bit like working for the Queen. We don't mind being God's servants. Clergy, of course, do it in a professional way, and they often gain rather than lose status because of their calling. There are the extra titles of respect like *Venerable* and *Doctor,* and places of honour at community gatherings. When the whole question of the ordination of women was gathering up a storm in our church a few years ago, my husband commented that there wouldn't be so much fuss about it if there were less talk about priesthood and authority, and more talk about ministry and service.

The problem begins in our own human nature, and Jesus had constantly to deal with it among his chosen group of twelve. James and John apparently prompted their mother to ask if they could have the best seats in the kingdom, and at the Last Supper not one of the twelve men who had been living with Jesus for three years had the grace to do the servant's task of washing feet when they came into the upper room. They all went to the meal with their hot, dry, dusty feet, until the master himself got out the towel and basin, and began to do the work for which they had been too proud.

All this sounds very well in theory, of course, but in practice it becomes a more difficult matter. There is the business of being taken for granted. Homemakers and mothers, for instance, don't get paid for their work, and most of the time they don't even get thanked. Nobody is going to congratulate you or admire you for deciding to be a servant. In fact, some people may even try to take advantage of you and quietly pass some of their work over to you.

Being God's servant means not expecting great rewards for our work. Jesus told a story about a servant who worked hard in the fields all day, came back to the house, cooked his master's supper, and then stood by him while he ate. And did the master thank the servant for doing what was commanded? No, said Jesus. "And you also, when you have done all that is commanded you, say, "We are unworthy servants; we have only done our duty."

Being God's servant means that although we may be asked to serve other people, we are not *their* servants. It means that we do the job that God has given us to do and nothing else. This is important because otherwise we may become overburdened with responsiblities of our own choosing, or that God has assigned to other people, and then our own job isn't done properly. If Mrs Jones in the office finds that she can rush through most of her day's work in a morning, she isn't doing the boss any favour if she begins to take on some of Miss Pretty's typing. Of course, Miss Pretty may be extremely grateful for the opportunity to take a longer lunch hour, but that is neither here nor there as far as the boss is concerned. In the same way, a mother may be conscientious about caring for her family, but she is neglecting her responsibility to teach her children how to be servants if they never have to make a bed or wash the dishes.

Being God's servant means learning to know the will of the Master through prayer and Bible study, setting our priorities according to these standards, and realizing that he never gives us more work than we can handle. When Jesus said that he called us friends rather than servants, he added that this was because servants don't know what the master is doing. But we do know.

Saint Paul wrote in his letter to the Galatians: "In love, be servants of one another." In any Christian community, in any Christian marriage, in any Christian family, the members should be servants of one another. When father and mother lovingly see to each other's needs, the children learn to have the same respect for their parents. And when parents lovingly care for their children, the children themselves are taught to care for each other. Example is the best teacher of all.

When I was a university student, I belonged to a Christian student group which had a campus-based "hang-out." It wasn't much of a meeting place – just a large basement room with a tiny kitchen, and another small room that served as an office for the chaplain. We used to meet there during the day with our friends just to talk and pass the time between lectures. We wasted a lot of time solving the affairs of the nation, while we lounged around drinking endless cups of coffee. Usually around four o'clock, someone would suddenly realize what time it was, and we would all dash off to a late afternoon lecture or the library. Always we left a coffee table piled high with dirty cups and saucers.

I won't say that I didn't feel a twinge of guilt the first time that I walked away from that coffee table. I did, but as I really was late for my lecture, there wasn't too much I could do about it. After that, I made sure that I left time to take *my* coffee cup into the kitchen and wash it before I left. Another girl followed my example, and it would be nice to say that everybody else got the same idea. But they didn't. The pile of dishes gathered on the table, and probably would have stayed there for weeks if some mysterious person hadn't done the dirty work. But every day when we came in, the coffee table was cleared and tidy, the room had been aired, and the clean coffee cups hung in neat rows above their saucers in the kitchen cupboard, waiting to be dirtied all over again.

It was some time before we discovered who the unseen servant was. The chaplain, it appeared, had been washing our cups every afternoon after we left, and those of us who were aware of the problem suddenly felt very ashamed. We girls had been resisting any impulse to do the dishes because we knew the guys in the group expected us to do them, and would be only too ready to pass it off as women's work. Now we had been humbled in a different way. It was at that point that I first began to understand what the foot-washing episode at the Last Supper was all about, and that looking after your own dirty cup simply isn't good enough.

O God
It's my nature
to love to be served,
to have that extra bit of attention.
Yet I know that I'll never
be really useful to you
till that human nature is changed.
May the Spirit of Jesus change me,
for He came not to be served
but to serve.
Then shall I find
a new freedom for service
in You.

"Jesus talked about a sweeping women" — *The Godswept Heart*.

First Steps

Like any young mother, I watched eagerly as my first baby learned to sit up and then to crawl. I was waiting with great anticipation for the magic moment when he would take his first steps. He was an active, energetic baby, and so inquisitive that I was sure he would be up and running about long before the average age for such activity. How right I was! At nine months he pulled himself up on a table leg and stepped out on his own. One tottery step followed another until he collapsed in a heap on the floor, but from then on he was mobile. And how mobile a nine-month baby can be defies comparison! He was on top of the piano, under the sink, into the medicine cabinet, and out the front door. I had my hands full.

More experienced mothers had said, "Don't be in such a hurry for him to walk. You'll be running after him soon enough." And I must admit that by the time we had our third child, I wasn't the least bit anxious to set any neighbourhood records for early walking.

Watching those first tumbling steps of my children made me realize why humility is such a great virtue. When we are low and close to the ground, there isn't a very long way to fall. We can afford to take risks and chances for God's sake that we might be afraid to try if we were tall and proud and self-sufficient. My older children dragged me out onto the skating rink one winter day, and although I had been a fairly proficient skater in my younger days, I found myself edging about the rink with some circumspection. It wasn't too many minutes before I lost my balance, and as I had thought, the ice was very hard and a long way down. It made me glad that I didn't need to learn how to walk at my present height and age.

It is fascinating to see a child grow and develop. First, he is so dependent on you. He needs to be picked up and carried wherever he goes. This may be a nuisance to a mother at times, but it does mean that she can put the baby where she wants him and he will stay there.

The baby learns to crawl and then to walk. He wants to explore, to find out everything. At first he is glad to hold your hand for the extra support, but then he lets go because he wants to run off on his own. All too soon there comes a time when you won't know where he is or what he is doing. Growing up is a process of "letting go," as the child lets go of his mother, and the mother lets go of her child.

Sometimes it seems to me that the spiritual life reverses this process. There we are running around doing our own thing, and we begin to be aware of the presence of God in our lives. From then on it is a matter of gradually leaving our independence behind and becoming more dependent on him. Growing up in the normal sense of the term means leaving mother and father behind in order to be independent. But growing up in Christ means almost the opposite, as we find God and become dependent, learning to know his will and to do it.

Jesus said that we must become "as little children" to enter the kingdom of heaven. He did not mean that we should go back to live in our parents' home, or revert to colouring with crayons and watching Sesame Street, any more than he meant Nicodemus to go back into his mother's womb in order to be "born again." He meant that we would have to leave our pride and our independence behind in order to dwell in our Father's house. We must learn to stay with him, to hold his hand for support, to wait for his permission when we want to go farther afield.

Just as there is no one stage of childhood, so there is no one stage of being the child of God. There are, of course, those who have moved right out of the house and live on their own, with a weekly phone call or a visit, and an occasional cry for help when they need financial or moral support. These are no longer little children.

Then there are the younger teen-agers who live at home but who are often fairly resistant about its restrictions. For them, peer group pressure can be very strong, and they care a lot about what their friends are doing and about what they will say.

The child in elementary school is much more centred on his home, although he too is under a lot of pressure from his friends to join the gang's activities. When my children were this age, I found they were in and out of the house a lot, just to go to the bathroom, or collect a catcher's mitt, or maybe to bring their friends in for juice and cookies. If they played somewhere else after school, at least I knew that they would be home for supper. They were always off on one project or another, but they usually came home again after a fairly short time.

For the toddler or pre-school child, home is nearly his whole world. His mother and father, his brothers and sisters, are the most important people in the world to him, and everyone else is a stranger. He likes being held and cuddled, and will sometimes take his mother's hand in a strange place, not because he needs support in standing up but because he is a little nervous.

And of course there is the baby, who has not learned to walk yet, who must be carried about, and who is almost completely helpless. Little babies need to be fed more frequently than the rest of us. They have to be bathed and dressed. They have to be put to bed, or put in the sun or fresh air. They are totally dependent on their parents for nurture and support.

It is difficult to understand, but this seems to be the long-term direction of our spiritual life, although only the saints seem to get that far. The typical Christian paradox is that Christian maturity is not maturity in the sense that we understand the term. It does not involve self-sufficiency and standing-on-your-own-feet. It doesn't mean being big enough and smart enough to make your own decisions. Instead Christian maturity, looked at from this perspective, appears to be an extreme type of immaturity, because it presupposes a total dependence on God for everything.

On the other hand, the mature Christian is not likely to give the impression of immaturity. Because he depends on God, he does not need to depend on other people. He may value the support and counsel of other Christians, but he is not dependent on them. If everyone should desert him and leave him to a lonely martyrdom, he will not change his mind and join the crowd. Held and supported by the God of all, what need does he have of human comfort? How many brave saints and martyrs have gone to the lions or stake in just that frame of mind! Jesus, in warning Saint Peter of his own martyr's death, said, "When you were young, you girded yourself and walked where you would; but when you are old, you will stretch out your hands, and another will gird you and carry you where you do not wish to go."

This process of getting smaller and humbler and less self-directed can be most clearly seen in the prayer life of a growing Christian. At first we are like the teen-agers who live at home but question the house rules, who may be prepared to talk things over with Mom and Dad while giving equal attention to what their friends say. There is a lot of hustle and bustle in our prayer-time because we are busy thinking about the claims of God on our lives and about what we can do for him.

Almost imperceptibly we may begin to move more completely under his rule and governance. We spend more time "at home" and are less likely to question his decisions regarding our lives and circumstances. God is always there in the background of our lives so that even though we may not be constantly at prayer, we are nevertheless in a close and comfortable relationship with him. We discuss with him our plans and ambitions, and if a door should suddenly close on a pet project, we are able to accept it as the wise guidance of a loving Father.

The biggest shift comes when other people and other concerns begin to lose their priority in our lives. God himself becomes uppermost in our thoughts, and his will becomes the main thrust of our own ambitions. We love others through him and in him, for his sake and not because of their own personal qualities, so that it becomes possible to love quite honestly the most difficult or unpleasant people.

In the life of prayer the spiritual masters speak of a kind of passivity which takes hold, allowing God himself to act in and upon us. As Saint Paul wrote: "The Spirit helps us in our weakness; for we do not know how to pray as we ought, but the Spirit himself intercedes for us with sighs too deep for words."

"Be still and know that I am God," wrote the Psalmist, for only when our desires and clamour of spirit are quieted can we know the infilling presence of God. And again, the Psalmist wrote:

"O Lord, my heart is not lifted up,
my eyes are not raised too high;
I do not occupy myself with things
too great and too marvelous for me.

But I have calmed and quieted my soul,
like a child quieted at its mother's breast;
like a child that is quieted is my soul.

O God
Of course I've known
what Jesus said
about being a little child,
yet I've always wanted
to be out in the forefront,
to lead the way,
to make real progress in the spiritual life,
to grow up in every way to Christ.
But so often I've got growing up
the wrong way round:
I've thought about what I could do,
and not about what you could do
in me
if only I would hand myself over
completely
to You.

"When we are low, there isn't a long way to fall" — *First Steps.*

Sky in the Pie

Some nameless wit once defined Christianity as *"pie in the sky when you die."* The obvious inference was that if you hang on through all the trials of day-to-day living, and take your licks with fairly good grace, and eat the things that are good for you, you'll get your reward in heaven.

However true this may be theologically, the fact remains that most of us aren't spiritually far-sighted enough to think that far ahead. Like a needy man with a welfare cheque, we tend to want some satisfaction, some rewards right away, just to break the dreariness of life. With life expectancies increasing every year, we simply aren't prepared to wait, nor is life generally so unbearable that we're willing to trade it in on what is essentially an unknown quantity.

This is where pie-in-the-sky theology breaks down. It really doesn't work all that well. One of the things I've noticed with my own family is that the best dessert in the world never makes up for an awful meal. We do take it as a general rule that anybody who isn't hungry enough to eat his or her dinner certainly doesn't need dessert. Yet even under these stringent conditions, German chocolate cake and pecan pie are no match at all for the horrors of fried fish, beets, and spinach at the same meal! Better to exist on plain bread and milk, or even go hungry, than try to plough through such a combination.

There was one momentous occasion in my own childhood when I did make such an effort. I don't happen to recall what the coveted dessert was, but I do remember the main course. It was liver and mashed turnips. I detested them both, and there seemed to be a veritable mountain of them on my plate. However, for the sake of dessert, I managed to gulp down every last mouthful. It was a short-lived triumph. Before my promised reward had even reached the table, I found myself making a frantic dash for the kitchen sink.

Somehow I suspect the same thing happens to Christians who try to choke down the difficulties of life for the sake of the reward they're going to get in heaven. Somewhere along the line it sticks in your throat. There seems to be something not quite right about living just for the reward, just for what we're going to get out of it. Life should have more meaning than that.

Quite apart from the fact that pie-in-the-sky doesn't work, this kind of thinking is also a very real distortion of Christian belief. Hopefully we're all headed for glory, but at the same time we have to remember that Jesus talked a lot more about having the kingdom of heaven *within* us. What we all need, and God wants to give us, is a little more sky in the pie we already have on our plate.

In my later years, although it had seemed impossible at the time, I actually came to like liver and turnips. It had started with lots of gravy on the meat and brown sugar on the turnips, and the time came when I not only tolerated but actually liked them. Without the gravy, without the sugar! Liver and turnips were foods I could eat and enjoy.

There are times when life seems to serve up a Blue Plate Special full of trouble. Really mature Christians say times like this are "good" for us. Taken properly, they are occasions for strengthening our faith and reassessing our priorities. Jesus talked about such times in that bewildering Sermon on the Mount, when he spoke about the "happiness" of the poor and the persecuted and the bereaved. Some happiness!

And yet it is in our need that God is able to bless us. It may not be proper to think of the Holy Spirit in terms of gravy or sugar, but I do know in a limited way what a difference God can make to the most depressing situation, if we only ask him. There are certainly plenty of Christians who have testified much more eloquently to the help he gives.

I'm not really sure that God expects us to learn to *like* being poor or persecuted or bereaved, although there are saints who claim to have acquired a taste for such things. It does seem important that we should learn "the secret of facing plenty and hunger, abundance and want," and so be able to say with Saint Paul that we can do anything through him who strengthens us. This is really living, without having to wait for any reward.

It is this ability to see ordinary things transfigured, to see the gold in the daily dust and the hand of God in all around us, that has marked out holy men and women through the ages. Jeremiah saw the word of the Lord in a flowering almond tree and in a cauldron on the fire. Jesus spoke in parables – about a woman who had lost a coin and swept until she found it, and about putting a lamp on a lampstand instead of hiding it away. Many others have used such homely illustrations, both in understanding great truths themselves, and in helping others to understand. The poet Angela Morgan spoke for many ordinary housewives when she wrote:

> I am aware
> As I go commonly sweeping the stair . . .
> I am aware of the splendour that ties
> All the things of the earth, with the things of the skies.

There really are sermons in stones, if we only have ears to hear, and also in new carpets and dirty windows and vacuum cleaners. Saint Teresa of Avila reminded her sisters that "the Lord walks among the pots and pans." Nothing is too small or insignificant for God to teach us a lesson. And along with this we also learn how all our activities that seem so inconsequential can attain an importance and significance beyond anything which we can imagine. If our prayers are to mean anything at all, they need to be backed up by the kind of lives we lead and the kind of people we are.

To think of heaven as a dessert, even as a particularly delicious dessert, puts the emphasis in the wrong place. Dessert is always an extra, something we can do without. If heaven is anything at all, it's the real substance of life, it's being "with the Lord." Jesus told us that he was the Bread of Heaven (not the Pie of Heaven) and he came among us to give us true life. For it is only as our lives are mingled in some way with the divine purpose that they have any real meaning and value.

O God
I never thought that you wanted to reward me.
I can't really say I deserve that!
Besides, it's just not the way you work,
like the driver dangling
the carrot before the donkey's nose.
Jesus talked about
finding the treasure.
I know that I shan't find it
in the things I possess
or even the things I have my eye on.
The clues to it are not in complicated theology
but in life around me.
It's in being open to you,
in relationships,
in doing the work you've given me to do,
even in suffering,
that I shall find the treasure.
For I know in my heart that
the treasure really
is You.